cupcakes & muffins
100 everyday recipes

First published in 2011
LOVE FOOD is an imprint of Parragon Books Ltd

Parragon
Queen Street House
4 Queen Street
Bath BA1 1HE, UK

ISBN. 978-1-4454-3041-6

Printed in China

Produced by Ivy Contract
Photography by Charlie Paul

Notes for the Reader

This book uses both metric and imperial measurements. Follow the same units of measurement throughout; do not mix metric and imperial. All spoon measurements are level: teaspoons are assumed to be 5 ml, and tablespoons are assumed to be 15 ml. Unless otherwise stated, milk is assumed to be full fat, eggs and individual vegetables are medium, and pepper is freshly ground black pepper.

The times given are an approximate guide only. Preparation times differ according to the techniques used by different people and the cooking times may also vary from those given. Optional ingredients, variations or serving suggestions have not been included in the calculations.

Recipes using raw or very lightly cooked eggs should be avoided by infants, the elderly, pregnant women, convalescents and anyone suffering from an illness. Pregnant and breastfeeding women are advised to avoid eating peanuts and peanut products. Sufferers from nut allergies should be aware that some of the ready-made ingredients used in the recipes in this book may contain nuts. Always check the packaging before use.

cupcakes & muffins

introduction

Muffins, cupcakes, biscuits, bars and traybakes are without doubt the most versatile sweet treat you can make. While a large cake looks impressive, especially if it is beautifully decorated with frosting, it can really only be eaten from a plate, probably with a dessert fork. An individual cake, on the other hand, will travel, making it ideal for putting in a lunch box, taking on a picnic, even just taken into the garden for a mid-morning or afternoon snack.

This really does not make an individual cake any less special, however, because – as you will discover when you start baking – these one-person treasures are packed full of the most sumptuous ingredients, from fresh or dried fruits to chocolate and nuts. We've even included an equally delicious 'healthy options' section so that you won't miss out if you are keeping an eye on your intake of fats and sugar.

Of course, practicality isn't always the first consideration, and there are plenty of ideas for making sweet treats with more than a hint of indulgence! Frostings, decorations and flavourings such as liqueurs turn a cake into a celebration, and we've included a section especially for those special occasions in life. The romantic at heart can chart a whole marriage in muffins, cupcakes and biscuits, from Valentine's day and the wedding day to the christening and the silver and golden wedding anniversaries, with all the birthday parties and other festive occasions along the way!

Baking is a great way to pass the time on a rainy day, and these recipes are ideal for children to help with — muffins and cupcakes need very little mixing, and take only minutes to cook. Children will love helping to decorate party cookies, fairy cakes, and cupcakes to celebrate Christmas, Easter and Halloween — and they will certainly love to eat them, too!

fruit & nut

apple streusel cupcakes

ingredients

makes 14

½ tsp bicarbonate of soda
280-g/10-oz jar apple sauce
4 tbsp butter, softened,
    or soft margarine
85 g/3 oz raw brown sugar
1 large egg, lightly beaten
175 g/6 oz self-raising flour
½ tsp ground cinnamon
½ tsp freshly ground nutmeg

topping

50 g/1¾ oz plain flour
50 g/1¾ oz raw brown sugar
¼ tsp ground cinnamon
¼ tsp freshly grated nutmeg
2½ tbsp butter

method

1 Put 14 paper baking cases in a muffin pan, or place
   14 double-layer paper cases on a baking sheet.

2 First make the topping. Put the flour, sugar, cinnamon
   and nutmeg in a bowl or in the bowl of a food
   processor. Cut the butter into small pieces, then either
   rub it in by hand or blend in the processor until the
   mixture resembles fine breadcrumbs. Set aside while
   you make the cakes.

3 To make the cupcakes, add the bicarbonate of soda to
   the jar of apple sauce and stir until dissolved. Put the
   butter and sugar in a bowl and beat together until light
   and fluffy. Gradually beat in the egg. Sift in the flour,
   cinnamon and nutmeg and, using a large metal spoon,
   fold into the mixture, alternating with the apple sauce.

4 Spoon the mixture into the paper cases. Sprinkle a little
   topping over each cupcake to cover the tops and press
   down gently.

5 Bake the cupcakes in a preheated oven, 180°C/350°F/
   Gas Mark 4, for 20 minutes or until well risen and
   golden brown. Leave the cakes for 2–3 minutes before
   serving warm or transfer to a wire rack to cool.

carrot & orange cupcakes with mascarpone frosting

ingredients

makes 12

8 tbsp butter, softened,
    or soft margarine
115 g/4 oz brown sugar
juice and finely grated rind
    of 1 small orange
2 large eggs, lightly beaten
175 g/6 oz carrots, grated
25 g/1 oz walnut pieces,
    roughly chopped
125 g/4½ oz plain flour
1 tsp ground mixed spice
1½ tsp baking powder

frosting
280 g/10 oz Mascarpone cheese
4 tbsp icing sugar
grated rind of 1 large orange

method

1 Put 12 muffin paper cases in a muffin pan.

2 Put the butter, sugar and orange rind in a bowl and beat together until light and fluffy. Gradually add the eggs, beating well after each addition. Squeeze any excess liquid from the carrots and add to the mixture with the walnuts and orange juice. Stir into the mixture until well mixed. Sift in the flour, mixed spice and baking powder and then, using a metal spoon, fold into the mixture. Spoon the mixture into the paper cases.

3 Bake the cupcakes in a preheated oven, 180°C/350°F/ Gas Mark 4, for 25 minutes or until well risen, firm to the touch and golden brown. Transfer to a wire rack to cool.

4 To make the frosting, put the Mascarpone cheese, icing sugar and orange rind in a large bowl and beat together until well mixed.

5 When the cupcakes are cold, spread a little frosting on top of each, swirling it with a round-bladed knife. Store the cupcakes in the refrigerator until ready to serve.

shredded orange cupcakes

ingredients

makes 12

6 tbsp butter, softened,
    or soft margarine
85 g/3 oz caster sugar
1 large egg, lightly beaten
85 g/3 oz self-raising flour
25 g/1 oz ground almonds
grated rind and juice of
    1 small orange

topping

1 orange
55 g/2 oz caster sugar
15 g/¹⁄₂ oz toasted flaked almonds

method

1 Put 12 paper baking cases in a muffin pan, or put 12 double-layer paper cases on a baking sheet.

2 Put the butter and sugar in a bowl and beat together until light and fluffy. Gradually beat in the egg. Add the flour, ground almonds and orange rind and, using a large metal spoon, fold into the mixture. Fold in the orange juice. Spoon the mixture into the paper cases.

3 Bake the cupcakes in a preheated oven, 180°C/350°F/ Gas Mark 4, for 20–25 minutes or until well risen and golden brown.

4 Meanwhile, make the topping. Using a citrus zester, pare the rind from the orange, then squeeze the juice. Put the rind, juice and sugar in a saucepan and heat gently, stirring, until the sugar has dissolved, then simmer for 5 minutes.

5 When the cupcakes have cooked, prick them all over with a skewer. Spoon a little warm syrup and rind over each cupcake, then sprinkle the flaked almonds on top. Transfer to a wire rack to cool.

variation

Replace the orange rind and juice with lemon rind and juice.

cranberry cupcakes

ingredients

makes 14

5½ tbsp butter, softened,
   or soft margarine
100 g/3½ oz caster sugar
1 large egg
2 tbsp milk
100 g/3½ oz self-raising flour
1 tsp baking powder
75 g/2¼ oz cranberries, frozen

method

1 Put 14 paper baking cases in a muffin pan, or place
   14 double-layer paper cases on a baking sheet.

2 Put the butter and sugar in a bowl and beat together
   until light and fluffy. Gradually beat in the egg, then stir
   in the milk. Sift in the flour and baking powder and,
   using a large metal spoon, fold them into the mixture.
   Gently fold in the frozen cranberries. Spoon the mixture
   into the paper cases.

3 Bake the cupcakes in a preheated oven, 180°C/350°F/
   Gas Mark 4, for 15–20 minutes or until well risen and
   golden brown. Transfer to a wire rack to cool.

blueberry cupcakes

ingredients

makes 12

125 g/4½ oz butter, softened
140 g/5 oz caster sugar
2 eggs, lightly beaten
140 g/5 oz plain flour
½ tsp baking powder
125 g/4½ oz ready-to-eat
    dried blueberries
2 tbsp milk
icing sugar, for dusting

method

1 Line a 12-hole muffin pan with 12 paper cases. Place
   the butter and sugar in a large bowl and beat together
   until light and fluffy, then gradually beat in the eggs.
   Sift in the flour and baking powder and fold into the
   mixture, then fold in the blueberries and milk. Spoon
   the mixture into the paper liners.

2 Bake in the preheated oven, 180°C/350°F/Gas Mark 4,
   for 25 minutes, or until golden brown and firm to the
   touch. Let the cupcakes cool in the pan for 10 minutes,
   then transfer to a wire rack to cool completely.

3 When the cupcakes are cold, dust the tops with sifted
   icing sugar.

coconut cherry cupcakes

ingredients

makes 12

8 tbsp butter, softened,
    or soft margarine
115 g/4 oz caster sugar
2 tbsp milk
2 eggs, lightly beaten
85 g/3 oz self-raising flour
½ tsp baking powder
85 g/3 oz dessicated coconut
115 g/4 oz glacé cherries,
    quartered
12 whole glacé, maraschino or
    fresh cherries, to decorate

frosting

4 tbsp butter, softened
115 g/4 oz icing sugar
1 tbsp milk

method

1 Put 12 paper baking cases in a muffin pan, or place
   12 double-layer paper cases on a baking sheet.

2 Put the butter and sugar in a bowl and beat together
   until light and fluffy. Stir in the milk. Gradually add the
   eggs, beating well after each addition. Sift in the flour
   and baking powder and fold them in with the coconut.
   Gently fold in most of the quartered cherries, then
   spoon the mixture into the paper cases and sprinkle
   the remaining quartered cherries over the top.

3 Bake the cupcakes in a preheated oven, 180°C/350°F/
   Gas Mark 4, for 20–25 minutes or until well risen,
   golden brown and firm to the touch. Transfer to a wire
   rack to cool.

4 To make the buttercream frosting, put the butter in
   a bowl and beat until fluffy. Sift in the icing sugar and
   beat together until well mixed, gradually beating in
   the milk.

5 To decorate the cupcakes, using a piping bag fitted
   with a large star tip, pipe a little frosting on top of each
   cupcake, then add a glacé, maraschino or fresh cherry
   to decorate.

tropical pineapple cupcakes with citrus cream frosting

ingredients

makes 12

2 slices of canned pineapple
  in natural juice
6 tbsp butter, softened,
  or soft margarine
85 g/3 oz caster sugar
1 large egg, lightly beaten
85 g/3 oz self-raising flour
1 tbsp juice from the canned
  pineapple

frosting

2 tbsp butter, softened
100 g/3½ oz soft cream cheese
grated rind of 1 lemon or lime
100 g/3½ oz icing sugar
1 tsp lemon juice or lime juice

method

1 Put 12 paper baking cases in a muffin pan, or place 12 double-layer paper cases on a baking sheet.

2 Finely chop the pineapple slices. Put the butter and sugar in a bowl and beat together until light and fluffy. Gradually beat in the egg. Add the flour and, using a large metal spoon, fold into the mixture. Fold in the chopped pineapple and the pineapple juice. Spoon the mixture into the paper cases.

3 Bake the cupcakes in a preheated oven, 180°C/350°F/ Gas Mark 4, for 20 minutes or until well risen and golden brown. Transfer to a wire rack to cool.

4 To make the frosting, put the butter and cream cheese in a large bowl and, using an electric hand whisk, beat together until smooth. Add the rind from the lemon or lime. Sift the icing sugar into the mixture, then beat together until well mixed. Gradually beat in the juice from the lemon or lime, adding enough to form a spreading consistency.

5 When the cupcakes are cold, spread a little frosting on top of each cake, or fill a piping bag fitted with a large star tip and pipe the frosting on top. Store the cupcakes in the refrigerator until ready to serve.

warm strawberry cupcakes baked in a teacup

ingredients

makes 6

8 tbsp butter, softened,
    plus extra for greasing
4 tbsp strawberry conserve
115 g/4 oz caster sugar
2 eggs, lightly beaten
1 tsp vanilla essence
115 g/4 oz self-raising flour
450 g/1 lb small whole fresh
    strawberries
icing sugar, for dusting

method

1 Grease 6 heavy, round teacups with butter. Spoon 2 teaspoons of the strawberry conserve in the bottom of each teacup.

2 Put the butter and sugar in a bowl and beat together until light and fluffy. Gradually add the eggs, beating well after each addition, then add the vanilla essence. Sift in the flour and, using a large metal spoon, fold it into the mixture. Spoon the mixture into the teacups.

3 Stand the cups in a roasting tin, then pour in enough hot water to come one-third of the way up the sides of the cups. Bake the cupcakes in a preheated oven, 180°C/350°F/Gas Mark 4, for 40 minutes or until well risen and golden brown and a skewer inserted in the centre comes out clean. If over-browning, cover the cupcakes with a sheet of foil. Leave the cupcakes to cool for 2–3 minutes, then carefully lift the cups from the tin and place them on saucers.

4 Place a few whole strawberries on each cake, then dust them with a little sifted icing sugar. Serve warm with the remaining strawberries.

moist walnut cupcakes

ingredients

makes 12

85 g/3 oz walnuts
4 tbsp butter, softened
100 g/3½ oz caster sugar
grated rind of ½ lemon
70 g/2½ oz self-raising flour
2 eggs
12 walnut halves, to decorate

frosting

4 tbsp butter, softened
85 g/3 oz icing sugar
grated rind of ½ lemon
1 tsp lemon juice

method

1 Put 12 paper baking cases in a muffin pan, or place 12 double-layer paper cases on a baking sheet.

2 Put the walnuts in a food processor and, using a pulsating action, blend until finely ground, being careful not to overgrind, which will turn them to oil. Add the butter, cut into small pieces, along with the sugar, lemon rind, flour and eggs, then blend until evenly mixed. Spoon the mixture into the paper cases.

3 Bake the cupcakes in a preheated oven, 190°C/375°F/ Gas Mark 5, for 20 minutes or until well risen and golden brown. Transfer to a wire rack to cool.

4 To make the frosting, put the butter in a bowl and beat until fluffy. Sift in the icing sugar, add the lemon rind and juice, and mix well.

5 When the cupcakes are cold, spread a little frosting on top of each cupcake and top with a walnut half to decorate.

banana & pecan cupcakes

ingredients

makes 24

225 g/8 oz plain flour
1¼ tsp baking powder
¼ tsp bicarbonate of soda
2 ripe bananas
8 tbsp butter, softened,
    or soft margarine
115 g/4 oz caster sugar
½ tsp vanilla essence
2 eggs, lightly beaten
4 tbsp sour cream
55 g/2 oz pecan nuts,
    roughly chopped

topping

8 tbsp butter, softened
115 g/4 oz icing sugar
25 g/1 oz pecan nuts,
    finely chopped

method

1 Put 24 paper baking cases in 2 muffin pans, or place
   24 double-layer paper cases on a baking sheet.

2 Sift together the flour, baking powder and bicarbonate
   of soda. Peel the bananas, put them in a bowl and
   mash with a fork.

3 Put the butter, sugar and vanilla in a bowl and beat
   together until light and fluffy. Gradually add the eggs,
   beating well after each addition. Stir in the mashed
   bananas and sour cream. Using a metal spoon, fold
   in the sifted flour mixture and chopped nuts, then
   spoon the mixture into the paper cases.

4 Bake the cupcakes in a preheated oven, 190°C/375°F/
   Gas Mark 5, for 20 minutes or until well risen and
   golden brown. Transfer to a wire rack to cool.

5 To make the topping, beat the butter in a bowl until
   fluffy. Sift in the icing sugar and mix together well.
   Spread a little topping on top of each cupcake
   and sprinkle with the finely chopped pecan nuts
   before serving.

frosted peanut butter cupcakes

ingredients

makes 16

4 tbsp butter, softened,
    or soft margarine
225 g/8 oz brown sugar
115 g/4 oz crunchy
    peanut butter
2 eggs, lightly beaten
1 tsp vanilla essence
225 g/8 oz plain flour
2 tsp baking powder
100 ml/3½ fl oz milk

frosting

200 g/7 oz full-fat soft
    cream cheese
2 tbsp butter, softened
225 g/8 oz icing sugar

method

1 Put 16 muffin paper cases in a muffin pan.

2 Put the butter, sugar and peanut butter in a bowl and beat together for 1–2 minutes, or until well mixed. Gradually add the eggs, beating well after each addition, then add the vanilla essence. Sift in the flour and baking powder and then, using a metal spoon, fold them into the mixture, alternating with the milk. Spoon the mixture into the paper cases.

3 Bake the cupcakes in a preheated oven, 180°C/350°F/ Gas Mark 4, for 25 minutes or until well risen and golden brown. Transfer to a wire rack to cool.

4 To make the frosting, put the cream cheese and butter in a large bowl and, using an electric hand whisk, beat together until smooth. Sift the icing sugar into the mixture, then beat together until well mixed.

5 When the cupcakes are cold, spread a little frosting on top of each cupcake, swirling it with a round-bladed knife. Store the cupcakes in the refrigerator until ready to serve.

peaches & cream cupcakes

ingredients

makes 12

400 g/14 oz canned peach slices
    in fruit juice
115 g/4 oz butter, softened
115 g/4 oz caster sugar
2 eggs, lightly beaten
115 g/4 oz self-raising flour
150 ml/5 fl oz double cream

method

1 Line a 12-hole muffin pan with 12 paper cases. Drain the peaches, reserving the juice. Set aside 12 small slices and finely chop the remaining slices.

2 Place the butter and sugar in a large bowl and beat together until light and fluffy. Gradually beat in the eggs. Sift in the flour and fold into the mixture. Fold in the chopped peaches and 1 tablespoon of the reserved juice. Spoon the batter into the paper cases.

3 Bake in a preheated oven, 180°C/350°F/Gas Mark 4, for 25 minutes, or until golden brown. Let the cupcakes cool in the tin for 10 minutes, then transfer to a wire rack to cool completely.

4 When ready to decorate, place the cream in a bowl and whip until soft peaks form. Spread the cream on top of the cupcakes, using a knife to form the cream into peaks. Place the reserved peach slices on top to decorate.

lemon & raspberry cupcakes

ingredients
makes 12

115 g/4 oz butter, softened
115 g/4 oz caster sugar
2 eggs, lightly beaten
115 g/4 oz self-raising flour
finely grated rind of 1 lemon
1 tbsp lemon curd
100 g/3½ oz fresh raspberries

topping
25 g/1 oz butter
1 tbsp soft light brown sugar
1 tbsp ground almonds
1 tbsp plain flour

method

1 Line a 12-hole bun tin with 12 paper cases. To make the topping, place the butter in a saucepan and heat gently until melted. Pour into a bowl and add the sugar, ground almonds and flour and stir together until combined.

2 To make the cupcakes, place the butter and sugar in a large bowl and beat together until light and fluffy, then gradually add the eggs. Sift in the flour and fold into the mixture. Fold in the lemon rind, lemon curd and raspberries. Spoon the mixture into the paper cases. Add the topping to cover the top of each cupcake and press down gently.

3 Bake in a preheated oven, 200°C/400°F/Gas Mark 6, for 15–20 minutes, or until golden brown and firm to the touch. Leave the cupcakes to cool for 10 minutes, then transfer to a wire rack to cool completely.

fresh raspberry cupcakes

ingredients

makes 12

275 g/9½ oz fresh raspberries
150 ml/5 fl oz sunflower oil
2 eggs
140 ml/5 oz caster sugar
½ tsp vanilla extract
275 g/9½ oz plain flour
¾ tsp baking soda

topping
150 ml/5 fl oz cream
12 fresh raspberries
small mint leaves, to decorate

method

1 Line a 12-hole muffin pan with 12 paper liners. Place the raspberries in a large bowl and crush lightly with a fork.

2 Place the oil, eggs, sugar and vanilla extract in a large bowl and whisk together until well combined. Sift in the flour and baking soda and fold into the mixture, then fold in the crushed raspberries. Spoon the mixture into the paper cases.

3 Bake in a preheated oven, 180°C/350°F/Gas Mark 4, for 30 minutes, or until golden brown and firm to the touch. Let the cupcakes cool in the pan for 10 minutes, then transfer to a wire rack to cool completely.

4 When ready to decorate, make the topping. Place the cream in a bowl and whip until soft peaks form. Spread the cream on top of the cupcakes, using a knife to smooth the cream. Top each cupcake with a raspberry and decorate with mint leaves.

tropical banana & passion fruit muffins

ingredients

makes 12

2 bananas
about 150 ml/5 fl oz milk
280 g/10 oz plain flour
1 tbsp baking powder
pinch of salt
115 g/4 oz light brown sugar
2 eggs
6 tbsp sunflower oil or 85 g/3 oz
    butter, melted and cooled
1 tsp vanilla extract
2 passion fruits
2 tbsp honey

method

1 Line a 12-hole muffin pan with 12 paper liners. Mash the bananas and put in a jug. Add enough milk to make the purée up to 250 ml/9 fl oz.

2 Sift together the flour, baking powder and salt into a large bowl. Stir in the sugar.

3 Place the eggs in a large jug or bowl and beat lightly, then beat in the banana and milk mixture, oil and vanilla extract. Make a well in the centre of the dry ingredients and pour in the beaten liquid ingredients. Stir gently until just combined; do not overmix. Spoon the mixture into the paper liners.

4 Bake in a preheated oven, 200°C/400°F/Gas Mark 6, for 20 minutes, or until well risen, golden brown, and firm to the touch. Let cool in the pan for 5 minutes, then transfer to a wire rack to cool completely.

5 Meanwhile, halve the passion fruits and spoon the pulp into a small saucepan. Add the honey and heat very gently until warmed through. Spoon on top of the muffins before serving.

toffee apple cakes

ingredients

makes 12

55 g/2 oz butter, plus extra
    for greasing
2 dessert apples
1 tbsp lemon juice
250 g/9 oz plain flour
2 tsp baking powder
1½ tsp ground cinnamon
70 g/2½ oz soft light brown sugar
100 ml/3½ fl oz milk
100 ml/3½ fl oz apple juice
1 egg, lightly beaten

topping

2 tbsp single cream
40 g/1½ oz soft light brown sugar
15 g/½ oz butter

method

1 Grease a 12-hole muffin pan. Core and coarsely grate
    one of the apples and set aside. Slice the remaining
    apple into 5 mm/¼ inch thick wedges and toss in the
    lemon juice. Sift together the flour, baking powder and
    cinnamon, then stir in the sugar and grated apple.

2 Place the butter in a saucepan and heat gently until
    melted, then mix with the milk, apple juice and egg.
    Stir the liquid mixture into the dry ingredients, mixing
    lightly until just combined.

3 Spoon the mixture into the muffin pan and arrange
    2 apple slices on top of each. Bake in a preheated oven,
    200°C/400°F/Gas Mark 6, for 20–25 minutes, or until
    risen, firm and golden brown. Run a knife around the
    edge of each cake to loosen, then transfer to a wire
    rack to cool completely.

4 For the topping, place all the ingredients in a small pan
    and heat, stirring, until the sugar is dissolved. Increase
    the heat and boil for 2 minutes, or until syrupy. Cool
    slightly, then drizzle over the cakes and leave to set.

apple & cinnamon muffins

ingredients

makes 6

85 g/3 oz plain wholewheat flour
70 g/2½ oz plain white flour
1½ tsp baking powder
pinch of salt
1 tsp ground cinnamon
40 g/1½ oz golden caster sugar
2 small eating apples, peeled,
    cored and finely chopped
125 ml/4 fl oz milk
1 egg, beaten
4 tbsp butter, melted

topping

12 brown sugar lumps, roughly
    crushed
½ tsp ground cinnamon

method

1 Place 6 muffin paper cases in a muffin pan.

2 Sift both flours, baking powder, salt and cinnamon
   together into a large bowl and stir in the sugar and
   chopped apples. Place the milk, egg and butter in a
   separate bowl and mix. Add the wet ingredients to the
   dry ingredients and gently stir until just combined.

3 Divide the mixture evenly between the paper cases.
   To make the topping, mix the crushed sugar lumps
   and cinnamon together and sprinkle over the muffins.

4 Bake in a preheated oven, 200°C/400°F/Gas Mark 6, for
   20–25 minutes or until risen and golden. Remove the
   muffins from the oven and serve warm or place them
   on a wire rack to cool.

fig & almond muffins

ingredients

makes 12

2 tbsp sunflower or peanut oil,
   plus extra for oiling (if using)
250 g/9 oz plain flour
1 tsp bicarbonate of soda
½ tsp salt
225 g/8 oz raw sugar
85 g/3 oz dried figs, chopped
115 g/4 oz almonds, chopped
200 ml/7 fl oz water
1 tsp almond essence
2 tbsp chopped almonds,
   to decorate

method

1 Oil a 12-cup muffin pan with sunflower oil, or line it with 12 muffin paper cases. Sift the flour, bicarbonate of soda and salt into a mixing bowl. Add the raw sugar and stir together.

2 In a separate bowl, mix the figs, almonds and remaining sunflower oil together. Then stir in the water and almond essence. Add the fruit and nut mixture to the flour mixture and gently stir together. Do not overstir – it is fine for it to be a little lumpy.

3 Divide the muffin mixture evenly between the 12 cups in the muffin pan or the paper cases (they should be about two-thirds full), then sprinkle over the remaining chopped almonds to decorate. Transfer to a preheated oven, 190°C/375°F/Gas Mark 5, and bake for 25 minutes or until risen and golden.

4 Remove the muffins from the oven and serve warm, or place them on a wire rack to cool.

cranberry & cheese muffins

ingredients

makes 18

butter, for greasing
225 g/8 oz plain flour
2 tsp baking powder
½ tsp salt
55 g/2 oz caster sugar
4 tbsp butter, melted
2 large eggs, lightly beaten
175 ml/6 fl oz milk
115 g/4 oz fresh cranberries
25 g/1 oz freshly grated
     Parmesan cheese

method

1 Lightly grease 2 x 9-cup muffin pans with butter.

2 Sift the flour, baking powder and salt into a mixing
   bowl. Stir in the caster sugar.

3 In a separate bowl, combine the butter, beaten eggs
   and milk, then pour into the bowl of dry ingredients.
   Mix lightly together until all of the ingredients are
   evenly combined, then stir in the fresh cranberries.

4 Divide the mixture evenly between the prepared
   18 cups in the muffin pans. Sprinkle the grated
   Parmesan cheese over the top. Transfer the pans to
   a preheated oven, 200°C/400°F/Gas Mark 6, and bake
   for 20 minutes or until the muffins are well risen and
   a golden brown colour.

5 Remove the muffins from the oven and let them cool
   slightly in the pans. Place the muffins on a wire rack
   and cool completely.

nectarine & banana muffins

ingredients

makes 12

75 ml/2½ fl oz sunflower or peanut oil, plus extra for oiling (if using)
250 g/9 oz plain flour
1 tsp bicarbonate of soda
¼ tsp salt
¼ tsp allspice
100 g/3½ oz caster sugar
55 g/2 oz shelled almonds, chopped
175 g/6 oz ripe nectarine, peeled and chopped
1 ripe banana, sliced
2 large eggs
75 ml/2½ fl oz thick natural or banana-flavoured yogurt
1 tsp almond essence

method

1 Oil a 12-cup muffin pan with sunflower oil, or line it with 12 muffin paper cases. Sift the flour, bicarbonate of soda, salt and allspice into a mixing bowl. Add the caster sugar and chopped almonds and stir together.

2 In a separate large bowl, mash the nectarine and banana together, then stir in the eggs, remaining sunflower oil, yogurt and almond essence. Add the mashed fruit mixture to the flour mixture and then gently stir together until just combined. Do not overstir the mixture – it is fine for it to be a little lumpy.

3 Divide the muffin mixture evenly between the 12 cups in the muffin pan or the paper cases (they should be about two-thirds full). Transfer to a preheated oven, 200°C/400°F/Gas Mark 6, and bake for 20 minutes or until risen and golden. Serve warm from the oven, or place them on a wire rack to cool.

tropical coconut muffins

ingredients
makes 12

1 tbsp sunflower or peanut oil,
   for oiling (if using)
250 g/9 oz plain flour
1 tsp baking powder
1 tsp bicarbonate of soda
½ tsp allspice
115 g/4 oz butter
225 g/8 oz brown sugar
2 large eggs, beaten
2 tbsp thick natural, banana or
   pineapple-flavoured yogurt
1 tbsp rum
1 ripe banana, sliced
75 g/2¾ oz canned pineapple
   rings, drained and chopped
55 g/2 oz dessicated coconut

topping
4 tbsp raw sugar
1 tsp allspice
25 g/1 oz dessicated coconut

method

1 Oil a 12-cup muffin pan with sunflower oil or line it with 12 muffin paper cases. Sift the flour, baking powder, bicarbonate of soda and allspice into a mixing bowl.

2 In a separate large bowl, cream together the butter and brown sugar, then stir in the eggs, yogurt and rum. Add the banana, pineapple and dessicated coconut and mix together gently. Add the pineapple mixture to the flour mixture and then gently stir together until just combined. Do not overstir the mixture – it is fine for it to be a little lumpy.

3 Divide the muffin mixture evenly between the 12 cups in the muffin pan or the paper cases (they should be about two-thirds full). To make the topping, mix the raw sugar and allspice together and sprinkle over the muffins. Sprinkle over the dessicated coconut, then transfer to a preheated oven, 200°C/400°F/Gas Mark 6.

4 Bake for 20 minutes or until risen and golden. Remove the muffins from the oven and serve warm, or place them on a wire rack to cool.

apple shortcakes

ingredients

makes 4

2 tbsp butter, cut into small pieces,
    plus extra for greasing
150 g/5½ oz plain flour, plus
    extra for dusting
½ tsp salt
1 tsp baking powder
1 tbsp caster sugar
50 ml/2 fl oz milk
icing sugar, for dusting

filling

3 dessert apples, peeled,
    cored and sliced
100 g/3½ oz caster sugar
1 tbsp lemon juice
1 tsp ground cinnamon
300 ml/10 fl oz water
150 ml/5 fl oz double cream,
    lightly whipped

method

1 Lightly grease a baking sheet. Sift the flour, salt and
   baking powder into a large bowl. Stir in the sugar, then
   add the butter and rub it in with your fingertips until
   the mixture resembles fine breadcrumbs. Pour in the
   milk and mix to a soft dough.

2 On a lightly floured work surface, knead the dough
   lightly, then roll out to 1-cm/½-inch thick. Stamp out
   4 circles, using a 5-cm/2-inch cutter. Transfer the circles
   to the prepared baking sheet.

3 Bake in a preheated oven, 220°C/425°F/Gas Mark 7,
   for 15 minutes, until the shortcakes are well risen and
   lightly browned. Set aside to cool.

4 To make the filling, place the apple, sugar, lemon juice
   and cinnamon in a saucepan. Add the water, bring to
   the boil and simmer, uncovered, for 5–10 minutes or
   until the apples are tender. Cool slightly, then remove
   the apples from the pan.

5 To serve, split the shortcakes in half. Place each bottom
   half on an individual serving plate and spoon on a
   quarter of the apple slices, then the cream. Place the
   other half of the shortcake on top. Serve dusted with
   icing sugar.

maple pecan tarts

ingredients

makes 12

pastry
150 g/5½ oz plain flour,
    plus extra for dusting
6 tbsp butter
55 g/2 oz golden caster sugar
2 egg yolks

filling
2 tbsp maple syrup
150 ml/5 fl oz double cream
115 g/4 oz golden caster sugar
pinch of cream of tartar
6 tbsp water
175 g/6 oz pecan nuts
12 pecan nut halves,
    to decorate

method

1 Sift the flour into a large bowl, then cut the butter into pieces and rub it into the flour using your fingertips until the mixture resembles breadcrumbs. Stir in the sugar, then stir in the egg yolks to make a smooth dough. Wrap in clingfilm and chill for 30 minutes.

2 On a floured work surface, roll out the pastry thinly, cut out circles and use to line 12 tartlet tins. Prick the bottoms and press a piece of foil into each tart case. Bake in a preheated oven, 200°C/400°F/Gas Mark 6, for 10–15 minutes or until light golden. Remove the foil and bake for a further 2–3 minutes. Cool on a wire rack.

3 To make the filling, mix together half the maple syrup and half the cream in a bowl. Place the sugar, cream of tartar and water in a saucepan over low heat and stir until the sugar dissolves. Bring to the boil and boil until light golden. Remove from the heat and stir in the maple syrup and cream mixture.

4 Return to the heat and cook to the 'soft ball' stage, when a little of the mixture forms a soft ball when dropped in cold water. Stir in the remaining cream and stand until warm. Brush the remaining maple syrup over the edges of the tarts. Place the pecans in the pastry cases, spoon in the toffee and top with a nut half. Cool and serve.

summer fruit tartlets

ingredients

makes 12

pastry
200 g/7 oz plain flour,
    plus extra for dusting
85 g/3 oz icing sugar
55 g/2 oz ground almonds
115 g/4 oz butter
1 egg yolk
1 tbsp milk

filling
225 g/8 oz cream cheese
icing sugar, to taste, plus extra
    for dusting
350 g/12 oz fresh summer fruits,
    such as red and whitecurrants,
    blueberries, raspberries and
    small strawberries

method

1 To make the pastry, sift the flour and icing sugar into
    a bowl. Stir in the ground almonds. Add the butter and
    rub in until the mixture resembles breadcrumbs. Add
    the egg yolk and milk and work in with a spatula, then
    mix with your fingers until the dough binds together.
    Wrap the dough in clingfilm and chill in the refrigerator
    for 30 minutes.

2 On a floured work surface, roll out the pastry and use
    to line 12 deep tartlet or individual brioche tins. Prick
    the bottoms. Press a piece of foil into each tartlet,
    covering the edges, and bake in a preheated oven,
    200°C/400°F/Gas Mark 6, for 10–15 minutes or until
    light golden brown. Remove the foil and bake for a
    further 2–3 minutes. Transfer to a wire rack to cool.

3 To make the filling, place the cream cheese and icing
    sugar in a bowl and mix together. Place a spoonful of
    filling in each tartlet case and arrange the fruit on top.
    Dust with sifted icing sugar and serve.

chocolate

jumbo chocolate chip cupcakes

ingredients

makes 8

7 tbsp soft margarine
100 g/3½ oz caster sugar
2 large eggs
100 g/3½ oz self-raising flour
100 g/3½ oz plain chocolate chips

method

1 Put 8 muffin paper cases in a muffin pan.

2 Put the margarine, sugar, eggs and flour in a large bowl and, using an electric hand whisk, beat together until just smooth. Fold in the chocolate chips. Spoon the mixture into the paper cases.

3 Bake the cupcakes in a preheated oven, 190°C/375°F/ Gas Mark 5, for 20–25 minutes or until well risen and golden brown. Transfer to a wire rack to cool.

variation

Replace the plain chocolate chips with 55 g/2 oz milk chocolate chips and 55 g/2 oz chopped hazelnuts.

soft-centred chocolate cupcakes

ingredients

makes 8

4 tbsp soft margarine
55 g/2 oz caster sugar
1 large egg
85 g/3 oz self-raising flour
1 tbsp cocoa powder
55 g/2 oz plain chocolate
icing sugar, for dusting

method

1 Put 8 paper baking cases in a muffin pan, or place 8 double-layer paper cases on a baking sheet.

2 Put the margarine, sugar, egg, flour and cocoa in a large bowl and, using an electric hand whisk, beat together until just smooth.

3 Spoon half of the mixture into the paper cases. Using a teaspoon, make an indentation in the centre of each cake. Break the chocolate evenly into 8 squares and place a piece in each indentation, then spoon the remaining cake mixture on top.

4 Bake the cupcakes in a preheated oven, 190°C/375°F/ Gas Mark 5, for 20 minutes or until well risen and springy to the touch. Leave the cupcakes for 2–3 minutes before serving warm, dusted with sifted icing sugar.

mocha cupcakes with whipped cream

ingredients

makes 20

2 tbsp instant espresso
 coffee powder
6 tbsp butter
85 g/3 oz caster sugar
1 tbsp honey
200 ml/7 fl oz water
225 g/8 oz plain flour
2 tbsp cocoa powder
1 tsp bicarbonate of soda
3 tbsp milk
1 large egg, lightly beaten

topping

225 ml/8 fl oz whipping cream
cocoa powder, sifted, for dusting

method

1 Put 20 paper baking cases in 2 muffin pans, or place 20 double-layer paper cases on 2 baking sheets.

2 Put the coffee powder, butter, sugar, honey and water in a saucepan and heat gently, stirring, until the sugar has dissolved. Bring to the boil, then reduce the heat and simmer for 5 minutes. Pour into a large heatproof bowl and cool.

3 When the mixture has cooled, sift in the flour and cocoa. Dissolve the bicarbonate of soda in the milk, then add to the mixture with the egg and beat together until smooth. Spoon the mixture into the paper cases.

4 Bake the cupcakes in a preheated oven, 180°C/350°F/ Gas Mark 4, for 15–20 minutes or until well risen and firm to the touch. Transfer to a wire rack to cool.

5 For the topping, whisk the cream in a bowl until it holds its shape. Just before serving, spoon a heaped teaspoonful of cream on top of each cake, then dust lightly with sifted cocoa. Store the cupcakes in the refrigerator until ready to serve.

devil's food cakes with chocolate frosting

ingredients

makes 18

3½ tbsp soft margarine
115 g/4 oz brown sugar
2 large eggs
115 g/4 oz plain flour
½ tsp bicarbonate of soda
25 g/1 oz cocoa powder
125 ml/4 fl oz sour cream

frosting

125 g/4½ oz plain chocolate
2 tbsp caster sugar
150 ml/5 fl oz sour cream

chocolate curls (optional)

100 g/3½ oz plain chocolate

method

1 Put 18 paper baking cases in a muffin pan, or put 18 double-layer paper cases on a baking sheet.

2 Put the margarine, sugar, eggs, flour, bicarbonate of soda and cocoa in a large bowl and, using an electric hand whisk, beat together until just smooth. Using a metal spoon, fold in the sour cream. Spoon the mixture into the paper cases.

3 Bake the cupcakes in a preheated oven, 180°C/350°F/Gas Mark 4, for 20 minutes or until well risen and firm to the touch. Transfer to a wire rack to cool.

4 To make the frosting, break the chocolate into a heatproof bowl. Set the bowl over a saucepan of gently simmering water and heat until melted, stirring occasionally. Remove from the heat and cool slightly, then whisk in the sugar and sour cream until combined. Spread the frosting over the tops of the cupcakes and set in the refrigerator before serving. If liked, serve decorated with chocolate curls made by shaving plain chocolate with a potato peeler.

tiny chocolate cupcakes with ganache frosting

ingredients

makes 20

4 tbsp butter, softened
55 g/2 oz caster sugar
1 large egg, lightly beaten
55 g/2 oz self-raising flour
2 tbsp cocoa powder
1 tbsp milk
20 chocolate-coated coffee beans,
   to decorate (optional)

frosting

100 g/3½ oz plain chocolate
100 ml/3½ fl oz double cream

method

1 Put 20 double-layer mini paper cases on two baking sheets.

2 Put the butter and sugar in a bowl and beat together until light and fluffy. Gradually beat in the egg. Sift in the flour and cocoa and then, using a metal spoon, fold them into the mixture. Stir in the milk. Fill a piping bag, fitted with a large plain tip, with the mixture. Pipe it into the paper cases, until they are half full.

3 Bake the cakes in a preheated oven, 190°C/375°F/ Gas Mark 5, for 10–15 minutes or until well risen and firm to the touch. Transfer to a wire rack to cool.

4 To make the frosting, break the chocolate into a saucepan and add the cream. Heat gently, stirring, until the chocolate has melted. Pour into a large heatproof bowl and, using an electric hand whisk, beat the mixture for 10 minutes or until thick, glossy and cool.

5 Fill a piping bag, fitted with a large star tip, with the frosting and pipe a swirl on top of each cupcake. Alternatively, spoon over the frosting. Chill in the refrigerator for 1 hour before serving. Serve decorated with a chocolate-coated coffee bean, if liked.

dark & white chocolate fudge cakes

ingredients

makes 20

200 ml/7 fl oz water
85 g/3 oz butter
85 g/3 oz caster sugar
1 tbsp golden syrup
3 tbsp milk
1 tsp vanilla extract
1 tsp bicarbonate of soda
225 g/8 oz plain flour
2 tbsp plain cocoa

topping

50 g/1¾ oz plain chocolate,
    broken into pieces
4 tbsp water
50 g/1¾ oz butter
50 g/1¾ oz white chocolate,
    broken into pieces
350 g/12 oz icing sugar
100 g/3½ oz plain chocolate
    shavings and 100 g/3½ oz
    white chocolate shavings,
    to decorate

method

1 Line two 12-hole muffin pans with 20 paper cases. Place the water, butter, sugar and syrup in a saucepan and heat gently, stirring, until the sugar has dissolved. Bring to a boil, reduce the heat and cook gently for 5 minutes. Let the syrup mixture cool.

2 Meanwhile, place the milk and vanilla extract in a bowl. Add the bicarbonate of soda and stir to dissolve. Sift the flour and cocoa into a separate bowl and add the syrup mixture. Stir in the milk mixture and beat until smooth, then spoon the batter into the paper cases.

3 Bake in a preheated oven, 180°C/350°F/Gas Mark 4, for 20 minutes, or until well risen and firm to the touch. Transfer to a wire rack to cool completely.

4 To make the topping, melt the plain chocolate with half the water and half the butter, in a small heatproof bowl set over a saucepan of gently simmering water. Stir until smooth and then leave to stand over the water. Repeat with the white chocolate and remaining water and butter. Sift half the icing sugar into each bowl and beat until smooth and thick. When the cupcakes are cold, top alternately with each icing, then let set. Decorate with chocolate shavings.

chocolate cherry cupcakes

ingredients

makes 12

50 g/1¾ oz plain chocolate,
    broken into pieces
60 g/2¼ oz butter
115 g/4 oz cherry jam
60 g/2¼ oz caster sugar
2 large eggs
100 g/3½ oz self-raising flour

topping

4 tsp kirsch liqueur
150 ml/5 fl oz double cream
12 fresh, glacé or maraschino
    cherries
chocolate shavings, to decorate

method

1 Line a 12-hole muffin pan with 12 paper cases. Place the chocolate and butter in a saucepan and heat gently, stirring continuously, until melted. Pour into a large bowl, then stir until smooth and let cool slightly. Add the jam, sugar and eggs to the cooled chocolate and beat together. Add the flour and stir together until combined. Spoon the batter into the paper cases.

2 Bake in a preheated oven, 180°C/350°F/Gas Mark 4, for 20 minutes, or until firm to the touch. Leave to cool in the pan for 10 minutes, then transfer to a wire rack to cool completely.

3 When the cupcakes are cold, sprinkle the kirsch over the top of each of the cakes and leave to soak for at least 15 minutes.

4 When ready to decorate, place the cream in a bowl and whip until soft peaks form. Spread the cream on top of the cupcakes with a knife to form the cream into peaks. Top each cupcake with a cherry and decorate with chocolate shavings.

chocolate fruit & nut crispy cakes

ingredients

makes 18

300 g/10½ oz plain chocolate, broken into pieces
150 g/5½ oz butter, cut into cubes
250 g/9 oz golden syrup
100 g/3½ oz Brazil nuts, coarsely chopped
100 g/3½ oz ready-to-eat dried raisins
200 g/7 oz cornflakes
18 glacé cherries, for decorating

method

1 Place 18 paper cases on a baking sheet. Place the chocolate, butter and dark corn syrup into a large saucepan and heat gently until the butter has melted and the ingredients are runny but not hot. Remove from the heat and stir until well mixed.

2 Add the chopped nuts and raisins to the pan and stir together until the fruit and nuts are covered in chocolate. Add the cornflakes and stir until combined.

3 Spoon the mixture evenly into the paper cases and top each with a glacé cherry. Leave to set in a cool place for 2–4 hours before serving.

chocolate butterfly cakes

ingredients

makes 12

8 tbsp soft margarine
100 g/3½ oz caster sugar
150 g/5½ oz self-raising flour
2 large eggs
2 tbsp cocoa powder
25 g/1 oz plain chocolate, melted
icing sugar, for dusting

filling

6 tbsp butter, softened
175 g/6 oz icing sugar
25 g/1 oz plain chocolate, melted

method

1 Put 12 paper baking cases in a muffin pan, or put 12 double-layer paper cases on a baking sheet.

2 Put the margarine, sugar, flour, eggs and cocoa in a large bowl and, using an electric hand whisk, beat together until just smooth. Beat in the melted chocolate. Spoon the mixture into the paper cases, filling them three-quarters full.

3 Bake the cupcakes in a preheated oven, 180°C/350°F/ Gas Mark 4, for 15 minutes or until springy to the touch. Transfer to a wire rack to cool completely.

4 To make the filling, put the butter in a bowl and beat until fluffy. Sift in the icing sugar and beat together until smooth. Add the melted chocolate and beat until well mixed.

5 When the cupcakes are cold, use a serrated knife to cut a circle from the top of each cake and then cut each circle in half. Spread or pipe a little of the buttercream into the centre of each cupcake and press the 2 semicircular halves into it at an angle to resemble butterfly wings. Dust with a little sifted icing sugar before serving.

dark chocolate & ginger muffins

ingredients

makes 12

6 tbsp sunflower oil or 85 g/3 oz
butter, melted and cooled,
plus extra for greasing
225 g/8 oz plain flour
55 g/2 oz cocoa powder
1 tbsp baking powder
1 tbsp ground ginger
pinch of salt
115 g/4 oz dark brown sugar
3 pieces stem ginger in syrup,
finely chopped, plus 2 tbsp
syrup from the jar
2 eggs
220 ml/7½ fl oz milk

method

1 Grease a 12-hole muffin tin. Sift together the flour,
cocoa, baking powder, ground ginger and salt into a
large bowl. Stir in the sugar and finely chopped stem
ginger.

2 Place the eggs in a large jug or bowl and beat lightly,
then beat in the milk, oil and ginger syrup. Make a
well in the centre of the dry ingredients and pour in
the beaten liquid ingredients. Stir gently until just
combined; do not overmix. Spoon the mixture into
the muffin tin.

3 Bake in a preheated oven, 200°C/400°F/Gas Mark 6, for
20 minutes, or until well risen and firm to the touch.
Leave to cool in the tin for 5 minutes, then serve warm
or transfer to a wire rack to cool completely.

rocky road chocolate muffins

ingredients

makes 12

6 tbsp sunflower oil or 85 g/3 oz
    butter, melted and cooled,
    plus extra for greasing
225 g/8 oz plain flour
55 g/2 oz cocoa power
1 tbsp baking powder
pinch of salt
115 g/4 oz caster sugar
100 g/3½ oz white chocolate chips
50 g/1¾ oz white mini
    marshmallows, cut in half
2 eggs
250 ml/9 fl oz milk

method

1 Grease a 12-hole muffin tin. Sift together the flour,
   cocoa powder, baking powder and salt into a
   large bowl. Stir in the sugar, chocolate chips and
   marshmallows.

2 Place the eggs in a large jug or bowl and beat lightly,
   then beat in the milk and oil. Make a well in the centre
   of the dry ingredients and pour in the beaten liquid
   ingredients. Stir gently until just combined; do not
   overmix. Spoon the batter into the muffin tin.

3 Bake in a preheated oven, 200°C/400°F/Gas Mark 6,
   for 20 minutes, or until risen and firm to the touch.
   Leave to cool in the tin for 5 minutes, then serve warm
   or transfer to a wire rack to cool completely.

chocolate chip muffins

ingredients

makes 12

3 tbsp soft margarine
200 g/7 oz caster sugar
2 large eggs
150 ml/5 fl oz whole natural
    yogurt
5 tbsp milk
300 g/10½ oz plain flour
1 tsp bicarbonate of soda
115 g/4 oz plain chocolate chips

method

1 Line a 12-cup muffin pan with muffin cases.

2 Place the margarine and sugar in a mixing bowl and beat with a wooden spoon until light and fluffy. Beat in the eggs, yogurt and milk until combined.

3 Sift the flour and bicarbonate of soda into the mixture. Stir until just blended.

4 Stir in the chocolate chips, then divide the mixture evenly between the paper cases and bake in a preheated oven, 200°C/400°F/Gas Mark 6, for 25 minutes or until risen and golden. Remove the muffins from the oven and cool in the pan for 5 minutes, then place them on a wire rack to cool completely.

spiced chocolate muffins

ingredients

makes 12

100 g/3½ oz butter, softened
150 g/5½ oz caster sugar
115 g/4 oz brown sugar
2 large eggs
150 ml/5 fl oz sour cream
5 tbsp milk
250 g/9 oz plain flour
1 tsp bicarbonate of soda
2 tbsp cocoa powder
1 tsp allspice
200 g/7 oz plain chocolate chips

method

1 Line a 12-cup muffin pan with muffin cases.

2 Place the butter, caster sugar and brown sugar in a bowl and beat well. Beat in the eggs, sour cream and milk until thoroughly mixed. Sift the flour, bicarbonate of soda, cocoa and allspice into a separate bowl and stir into the mixture. Add the chocolate chips and mix together well. Divide the mixture evenly between the paper cases.

3 Bake in a preheated oven, 190°C/375°F/Gas Mark 5, for 25–30 minutes. Remove from the oven and cool for 10 minutes, then transfer to a wire rack to cool completely. Store in an airtight container until required.

double chocolate muffins

ingredients

makes 12

200 g/7 oz plain flour
25 g/1 oz cocoa powder,
   plus extra for dusting
1 tbsp baking powder
1 tsp ground cinnamon
115 g/4 oz golden caster sugar
185 g/6½ oz white chocolate,
   broken into pieces
2 large eggs
100 ml/3½ fl oz sunflower
   or peanut oil
200 ml/7 fl oz milk

method

1 Line a 12-cup muffin pan with muffin cases.

2 Sift the flour, cocoa, baking powder and cinnamon into a large mixing bowl. Stir in the sugar and 125 g/4½ oz of the white chocolate.

3 Place the eggs and oil in a separate bowl and whisk until frothy, then gradually whisk in the milk. Stir into the dry ingredients until just blended. Divide the mixture evenly between the paper cases, filling each three-quarters full.

4 Bake in a preheated oven, 200°C/400°F/Gas Mark 6, for 20 minutes or until well risen and springy to the touch. Remove the muffins from the oven, cool in the pan for 2 minutes, then transfer to a wire rack to cool completely.

5 Place the remaining white chocolate in a heatproof bowl, set the bowl over a saucepan of barely simmering water, and heat until melted. Spread over the top of the muffins. Allow to set, then dust the tops with a little cocoa and serve.

chocolate orange muffins

ingredients

makes 9

sunflower or peanut oil,
    for oiling
150 g/5½ oz self-raising
    white flour
150 g/5½ oz self-raising
    wholewheat flour
55 g/2 oz ground almonds
55 g/2 oz brown sugar
rind and juice of 1 orange
175 g/6 oz cream cheese
2 large eggs
55 g/2 oz plain chocolate chips

method

1 Thoroughly oil a 9-cup muffin pan.

2 Sift both flours into a mixing bowl and stir in the ground almonds and sugar.

3 Mix the orange rind and juice, cream cheese and eggs together in a separate bowl. Make a well in the centre of the dry ingredients and stir in the wet ingredients, then add the chocolate chips. Beat well to combine all the ingredients.

4 Divide the mixture between the cups, filling each no more than three-quarters full. Bake in a preheated oven, 190°C/375°F/Gas Mark 5, for 20–25 minutes or until well risen and golden brown.

5 Remove the muffins from the oven and cool slightly on a wire rack, but eat them as fresh as possible.

mocha brownies

ingredients

makes 16

55 g/2 oz butter, plus extra
for greasing
115 g/4 oz plain chocolate,
broken into pieces
175 g/6 oz brown sugar
2 eggs
1 tbsp instant coffee powder,
dissolved in 1 tbsp hot water,
cooled
85 g/3 oz plain flour
½ tsp baking powder
55 g/2 oz roughly chopped
pecan nuts

method

1 Grease and line the bottom of a 20-cm/8-inch square cake tin. Place the butter and chocolate in a heavy-based saucepan over low heat until melted. Stir and set aside to cool.

2 Place the sugar and eggs in a large bowl and cream together until light and fluffy. Fold in the chocolate mixture and cooled coffee and mix thoroughly. Sift in the flour and baking powder and lightly fold into the mixture, then carefully fold in the pecan nuts.

3 Pour the mixture into the prepared tin and bake in a preheated oven, 180°C/350°F/Gas Mark 4, for 25–30 minutes or until firm and a skewer inserted into the centre comes out clean.

4 Cool in the tin for a few minutes, then run a knife round the edge of the cake to loosen it. Turn the cake out onto a wire rack and peel off the lining paper. Cool completely and when cold, cut into squares.

cappuccino squares

ingredients

makes 15

225 g/8 oz butter, softened,
    plus extra for greasing
225 g/8 oz self-raising flour
1 tsp baking powder
1 tsp cocoa powder,
    plus extra for dusting
225 g/8 oz golden caster sugar
4 eggs, beaten
3 tbsp instant coffee powder,
    dissolved in 2 tbsp hot water

frosting

115 g/4 oz white chocolate,
    broken into pieces
55 g/2 oz butter, softened
3 tbsp milk
175 g/6 oz icing sugar

method

1 Grease and line the bottom of a shallow 28 x 18-cm/
   11 x 7-inch tin. Sift the flour, baking powder and cocoa
   into a bowl and add the butter, caster sugar, eggs and
   coffee. Beat well, by hand or with an electric whisk, until
   smooth, then spoon into the tin and smooth the top.

2 Bake in a preheated oven, 180°C/350°F/Gas Mark 4, for
   35–40 minutes or until risen and firm. Cool in the tin
   for 10 minutes, then turn out onto a wire rack, peel
   off the lining paper and cool completely. To make the
   frosting, place the chocolate, butter and milk in a bowl
   set over a saucepan of simmering water and stir until
   the chocolate has melted.

3 Remove the bowl from the pan and sift in the icing
   sugar. Beat until smooth, then spread over the cake.
   Dust the top of the cake with sifted cocoa, then cut
   into squares.

chocolate tartlets

ingredients

makes 4

10 oz/275 g ready-made sweet
    pastry
150 g/5½ oz bittersweet chocolate,
    broken into pieces
50 g/1¾ oz butter
100 ml/3½ fl oz whipping cream
1 large egg
25 g/1 oz caster sugar
cocoa powder and chocolate curls,
    to decorate
crème fraîche, to serve

method

1 Roll out the pastry and use to line 4 x 12-cm/4½-inch
fluted tart tins with removable bases. Line these with
waxed paper, then fill with baking beans. Place on a
preheated baking sheet and bake in a preheated oven,
200°C/400°F/Gas Mark 6, for 5 minutes. Remove the
paper and beans and return the pastry shells to the
oven for 5 minutes. Remove from the oven, then
set aside on the baking sheet. Reduce the oven
temperature to 180°C/350°F/Gas Mark 4.

2 Meanwhile, place the chocolate in a bowl set over a
saucepan of simmering water so that the bowl does
not touch the water. Add the butter and cream and
heat until the chocolate and butter melt. Remove
from the heat.

3 Beat the egg and sugar together until light and fluffy.
Stir the melted chocolate mixture until smooth, then
stir it into the egg mixture. Carefully pour the filling
into the tart cases, then transfer to the oven and bake
for 15 minutes or until the filling is set and the pastry
is golden brown. If the pastry looks as though it is
becoming too brown, cover it with foil.

4 Transfer the tartlets to a wire rack to cool completely.
Dust with cocoa powder, decorate with chocolate
curls, and serve with the crème fraîche.

caramel chocolate shortbread

ingredients

makes 12

115 g/4 oz butter, plus extra
for greasing
175 g/6 oz plain flour
55 g/2 oz golden caster sugar

filling and topping

175 g/6 oz butter
115 g/4 oz golden caster sugar
3 tbsp golden syrup
400 g/14 oz canned condensed
milk
200 g/7 oz plain chocolate, broken
into pieces

method

1 Grease and line the bottom of a 23-cm/9-inch shallow square cake tin. Place the butter, flour and sugar in a food processor and process until it starts to bind together. Press into the pan and level the top. Bake in a preheated oven, 180°C/350°F/Gas Mark 4, for 20–25 minutes or until golden.

2 Meanwhile, make the caramel. Place the butter, sugar, syrup and condensed milk in a heavy-based saucepan. Heat gently until the sugar has melted. Bring to the boil, then reduce the heat and simmer for 6–8 minutes, stirring, until very thick. Pour over the shortbread and chill in the refrigerator for 2 hours, or until firm.

3 Melt the chocolate and allow to cool a little, then spread over the caramel. Chill in the refrigerator for 2 hours, or until set. Cut the shortbread into 12 pieces using a sharp knife and serve.

double chocolate chip cookies

ingredients

makes 12

200 g/7 oz butter, softened,
    plus extra for greasing
200 g/7 oz golden caster sugar
½ tsp vanilla essence
1 large egg
225 g/8 oz plain flour
pinch of salt
1 tsp bicarbonate of soda
115 g/4 oz white chocolate chips
115 g/4 oz plain chocolate chips

method

1 Place the butter, sugar and vanilla essence in a large bowl and beat together. Gradually beat in the egg until the mixture is light and fluffy.

2 Sift the flour, salt and bicarbonate of soda over the mixture and fold in. Fold in the chocolate chips. Drop dessertspoonfuls of the mixture onto 3 greased baking sheets, spaced well apart to allow for spreading during cooking.

3 Bake in a preheated oven, 180°C/350°F/Gas Mark 4, for 10–12 minutes or until crisp outside but still soft inside. Cool on the baking sheets for 2 minutes, then transfer to wire racks to cool completely.

special occasions

easter cupcakes

ingredients
makes 12

8 tbsp butter, softened,
    or soft margarine
115 g/4 oz caster sugar
2 eggs, lightly beaten
85 g/3 oz self-raising flour
25 g/1 oz cocoa powder

topping
6 tbsp butter, softened
175 g/6 oz icing sugar
1 tbsp milk
2–3 drops of vanilla essence
36 mini sugar-coated
    chocolate eggs, to decorate

method

1 Put 12 paper baking cases in a muffin pan, or place
   12 double-layer paper cases on a baking sheet.

2 Put the butter and sugar in a bowl and beat together
   until light and fluffy. Gradually add the eggs, beating
   well after each addition. Sift in the flour and cocoa and,
   using a large metal spoon, fold into the mixture. Spoon
   the mixture into the paper cases.

3 Bake the cupcakes in a preheated oven, 180°C/350°F/
   Gas Mark 4, for 15–20 minutes or until well risen and
   firm to the touch. Transfer to a wire rack to cool.

4 To make the buttercream topping, put the butter in
   a bowl and beat until fluffy. Sift in the icing sugar and
   beat together until well mixed, adding the milk and
   vanilla essence.

5 When the cupcakes are cold, put the frosting in a
   piping bag fitted with a large star tip and pipe a circle
   around the edge of each cupcake to form a nest.
   Place 3 chocolate eggs in the centre of each nest,
   to decorate.

springtime cupcakes

ingredients

makes 24

150 g/5½ oz butter, softened,
    or soft margarine
150 g/5½ oz caster sugar
1 tsp vanilla extract
2 large eggs, lightly beaten
140 g/5 oz self-raising flour
40 g/1½ oz cornflour

topping

115 g/4 oz ready-to-roll
    fondant icing
yellow and green food colourings
300 g/10½ oz icing sugar
about 3 tbsp cold water
coloured sugar strands

method

1 Line two 12-hole muffin pans with 24 paper cases.
Place the butter and sugar in a large bowl and beat
together until light and fluffy, then beat in the vanilla
extract. Gradually beat in the eggs. Sift in the flour
and cornflour and fold into the batter. Spoon the
batter into the paper cases. Bake in a preheated oven,
190°C/375°F/Gas Mark 5, for 12–15 minutes, or until
golden and springy to the touch. Transfer to a wire
rack to cool completely.

2 To decorate, divide the fondant in half and colour
one half pale yellow. Roll out both halves, then use
the sides of a round pastry cutter to cut out white
and yellow petal shapes. Set aside.

3 Sift the icing sugar into a bowl and mix with the water
until smooth. Place half of the icing in a small piping
bag fitted with a plain nozzle. Divide the icing in half
and colour one portion yellow and the other green.

4 Cover 12 cakes with yellow icing and 12 with green
icing. Arrange white petals on top of the yellow icing
to form flowers. Pipe a little blob of white icing into
the centre of each flower, then add a few coloured
sprinkles on top of the white icing to form the centre
of the flower. Arrange the yellow petals on the green
icing and decorate in the same way. Leave to set.

halloween cupcakes

ingredients

makes 12

8 tbsp soft margarine
115 g/4 oz caster sugar
2 eggs
115 g/4 oz self-raising flour

topping

200 g/7 oz orange ready-to-roll
    coloured fondant icing
icing sugar, for dusting
55 g/2 oz black ready-to-roll
    coloured fondant icing
black cake writing icing
white cake writing icing

method

1 Put 12 paper baking cases in a muffin pan, or place 12 double-layer paper cases on a baking sheet.

2 Put the margarine, sugar, eggs and flour in a bowl and, using an electric hand whisk, beat together until smooth. Spoon the mixture into the cases.

3 Bake the cupcakes in a preheated oven, 180°C/350°F/ Gas Mark 4, for 15–20 minutes or until well risen, golden brown and firm to the touch. Transfer to a wire rack to cool.

4 Knead the orange icing until pliable, then roll out on a work surface dusted with icing sugar. Using the palm of your hand, lightly rub icing sugar into the icing to prevent it from spotting. Using a 5.5-cm/2¼-inch plain round cutter, cut out 12 circles, rerolling the icing as necessary. Place a circle on top of each cupcake.

5 Roll out the black icing on a work surface lightly dusted with icing sugar. Using the palm of your hand, lightly rub icing sugar into the icing to prevent it from spotting. Using a 3-cm/1¼-inch plain round cutter, cut out 12 circles and place them on the centre of the cupcakes. Using black writing icing, pipe 8 legs on to each spider and using white writing icing, draw 2 eyes and a mouth.

christmas cupcakes

ingredients

makes 16

9 tbsp butter, softened
200 g/7 oz caster sugar
4–6 drops almond essence
4 eggs, lightly beaten
150 g/5½ oz self-raising flour
175 g/6 oz ground almonds

topping

450 g/1 lb white ready-to-roll
    fondant icing
55 g/2 oz green ready-to-roll
    coloured fondant icing
25 g/1 oz red ready-to-roll
    coloured fondant icing
icing sugar, for dusting

method

1 Put 16 paper muffin cases in a muffin pan. Put the butter, sugar and almond essence in a bowl and beat together until light and fluffy. Gradually add the eggs, beating well after each addition. Add the flour and, using a large metal spoon, fold it into the mixture, then fold in the ground almonds. Spoon the mixture into the paper cases to half-fill them.

2 Bake the cupcakes in a preheated oven, 180°C/350°F/ Gas Mark 4, for 20 minutes or until well risen, golden brown and firm to the touch. Transfer to a wire rack to cool.

3 Knead the white icing until pliable, then roll out on a work surface lightly dusted with icing sugar. Using a 7-cm/2¾-inch plain round cutter, cut out 16 circles, rerolling as necessary. Place a circle on each cupcake.

4 Roll out the green icing on a work surface lightly dusted with icing sugar. Using the palm of your hand, rub icing sugar into the frosting to prevent it from spotting. Using a holly leaf-shaped cutter, cut out 32 leaves, rerolling the icing as necessary. Brush each leaf with a little cooled boiled water and place 2 leaves on top of each cake. Roll the red icing between the palms of your hands to form 48 berries and place in the centre of the leaves.

valentine heart cupcakes

ingredients

makes 6

6 tbsp butter, softened, or soft margarine
85 g/3 oz caster sugar
½ tsp vanilla essence
2 eggs, lightly beaten
70 g/2½ oz plain flour
1 tbsp cocoa powder
1 tsp baking powder

marzipan hearts

35 g/1¼ oz marzipan
red food colouring (liquid or paste)
icing sugar, for dusting

topping

4 tbsp butter, softened
115 g/4 oz icing sugar
25 g/1 oz plain chocolate, melted
6 chocolate flower decorations

method

1 To make the hearts, knead the marzipan until pliable, then add a few drops of red colouring and knead until evenly coloured red. Roll out the marzipan to a thickness of 5 mm/¼ inch on a work surface dusted with icing sugar. Using a small heart-shaped cutter, cut out 6 hearts. Place on a tray lined with waxed paper and dusted with icing sugar. Set aside to dry for 3–4 hours.

2 Put 6 paper muffin cases in a muffin pan.

3 Put the butter, sugar and vanilla essence in a bowl and beat together until light and fluffy. Gradually add the eggs, beating well after each addition. Sift in the flour, cocoa and baking powder and, using a large metal spoon, fold into the mixture. Spoon the mixture into the paper cases.

4 Bake the cupcakes in a preheated oven, 180°C/350°F/Gas Mark 4, for 20–25 minutes or until well risen and firm to the touch. Transfer to a wire rack to cool.

5 To make the topping, put the butter in a large bowl and beat until fluffy. Sift in the icing sugar and beat together until smooth. Add the melted chocolate and beat together until well mixed. When the cakes are cold, spread a little topping on top of each cake and decorate with a marzipan heart and a chocolate flower.

cupcake wedding cake

ingredients

makes 48

450 g/1 lb butter, softened
450 g/1 lb caster sugar
2 tsp vanilla essence
8 large eggs, lightly beaten
450 g/1 lb self-raising flour
150 ml/5 fl oz milk

topping

550 g/1 lb 4 oz icing sugar
48 ready-made sugar roses, or
    48 small fresh rosebuds gently
    rinsed and left to dry on
    kitchen paper

to assemble the cake

one 50-cm/20-inch,
    one 40-cm/16-inch,
    one 30-cm/12-inch and
    one 20-cm/8-inch sandblasted
    glass disk with polished edges,
    or 4 silver cake boards
13 white or Perspex cake pillars
1 small bouquet of fresh flowers in
    a small vase

method

1 Put 48 paper baking cases in a muffin pan, or place 48 double-layer paper cases on a baking sheet. Put the butter, sugar and vanilla essence in a bowl and beat together until light and fluffy. Gradually add the eggs, beating well after each addition. Add the flour and, using a large metal spoon, fold into the mixture with the milk. Spoon the mixture into the paper cases.

2 Bake the cupcakes in a preheated oven, 180°C/350°F/ Gas Mark 4, for 15–20 minutes or until well risen and firm to the touch. Transfer to a wire rack to cool.

3 To make the topping, sift the icing sugar into a large bowl. Add 3–4 tablespoons hot water and stir until the mixture is smooth and thick enough to coat the back of a wooden spoon. Spoon a little on top of each cupcake. Store in an airtight container for one day.

4 On the day of serving, carefully place a sugar rose or rosebud on top of each cupcake. To arrange the cupcakes, place the largest disk or board on a table where the finished display is to be. Stand 5 pillars on the disk and arrange some of the cupcakes on the base. Continue with the remaining bases, pillars (using only 4 pillars to support each remaining tier), and cupcakes to make 4 tiers, standing the bouquet of flowers in the centre of the top tier.

rose petal cupcakes

ingredients

makes 12

8 tbsp butter, softened
115 g/4 oz caster sugar
2 eggs, lightly beaten
1 tbsp milk
few drops of extract of rose oil
¼ tsp vanilla essence
175 g/6 oz self-raising flour

frosting

6 tbsp butter, softened
175 g/6 oz icing sugar
pink or purple food colouring
    (optional)
silver dragées (cake decoration
    balls), to decorate

candied rose petals

12–24 rose petals
lightly beaten egg white,
    for brushing
caster sugar, for sprinkling

method

1 To make the candied rose petals, gently rinse the petals and dry well with kitchen paper. Using a pastry brush, paint both sides of a rose petal with egg white, then coat well with caster sugar. Place on a tray and repeat with the remaining petals. Cover the tray with foil and set aside to dry overnight.

2 Put 12 paper baking cases in a muffin pan, or place 12 double-layer paper cases on a baking sheet.

3 Put the butter and sugar in a bowl and beat together until light and fluffy. Gradually add the eggs, beating well after each addition. Stir in the milk, rose oil extract and vanilla essence then, using a metal spoon, fold in the flour. Spoon the mixture into the paper cases.

4 Bake the cupcakes in a preheated oven, 200°C/400°F/ Gas Mark 6, for 12–15 minutes or until well risen and golden brown. Transfer to a wire rack to cool.

5 To make the frosting, put the butter in a large bowl and beat until fluffy. Sift in the icing sugar and mix well together. If wished, add a few drops of pink or purple food colouring to complement the rose petals.

6 When the cupcakes are cold, spread a little frosting on top of each cake. Top with 1–2 candied rose petals and sprinkle with silver dragées to decorate.

lemon butterfly cakes

ingredients

makes 12

115 g/4 oz self-raising flour
½ tsp baking powder
8 tbsp soft margarine
115 g/4 oz caster sugar
2 eggs, lightly beaten
finely grated rind of ½ lemon
2 tbsp milk
icing sugar, for dusting

filling

6 tbsp butter, softened
175 g/6 oz icing sugar
1 tbsp lemon juice

method

1 Put 12 paper baking cases in a muffin pan, or place 12 double-layer paper cases on a baking sheet. Sift the flour and baking powder into a large bowl. Add the margarine, sugar, eggs, lemon rind and milk and, using an electric hand whisk, beat together until smooth. Spoon the mixture into the paper cases.

2 Bake the cupcakes in a preheated oven, 190°C/375°F/ Gas Mark 5, for 15–20 minutes or until well risen and golden brown. Transfer to a wire rack to cool.

3 To make the filling, put the butter in a bowl and beat until fluffy. Sift in the icing sugar, add the lemon juice and beat together until smooth and creamy.

4 When the cupcakes are cold, use a serrated knife to cut a circle from the top of each cupcake and then cut each circle in half. Spread or pipe a little of the buttercream filling into the centre of each cupcake, then press the 2 semicircular halves into it at an angle, to resemble butterfly wings. Dust with a little sifted icing sugar before serving.

variation

Omit the lemon rind from the cake mixture and replace the lemon juice in the icing with 1 teaspoon of vanilla extract

christening cupcakes

ingredients

makes 24

400 g/14 oz butter, softened
400 g/14 oz caster sugar
finely grated rind of 2 lemons
8 eggs, lightly beaten
400 g/14 oz self-raising flour

topping

350 g/12 oz icing sugar
red or blue food colouring
    (liquid or paste)
24 sugared almonds

method

1 Put 24 paper muffin cases in a muffin pan.

2 Put the butter, sugar and lemon rind in a bowl and beat together until light and fluffy. Gradually add the eggs, beating well after each addition. Add the flour and, using a large metal spoon, fold into the mixture. Spoon the lemon mixture into the paper cases to half-fill them.

3 Bake the cupcakes in a preheated oven, 180°C/350°F/ Gas Mark 4, for 20–25 minutes or until well risen, golden brown and firm to the touch. Transfer to a wire rack to cool.

4 When the cakes are cold, make the topping. Sift the icing sugar into a bowl. Add 6–8 teaspoons of hot water and stir until the mixture is smooth and thick enough to coat the back of a wooden spoon. Dip a skewer into the red or blue food colouring, then stir it into the icing until it is evenly coloured pale pink or pale blue.

5 Spoon a little icing on top of each cupcake. Top each with a sugared almond and allow to set for about 30 minutes before serving.

birthday party cupcakes

ingredients

makes 24

225 g/8 oz soft margarine
225 g/8 oz caster sugar
4 eggs
225 g/8 oz self-raising flour

topping

175 g/6 oz butter, softened
350 g/12 oz icing sugar
a variety of edible sugar flower
　　shapes, cake decorating
　　sprinkles, silver dragées
　　(cake decoration balls),
　　and sugar strands
various coloured tubes of writing
　　frosting
24 birthday cake candles (optional)

method

1 Put 24 paper baking cases in a muffin pan, or place 24 double-layer paper cases on a baking sheet.

2 Put the margarine, sugar, eggs and flour in a large bowl and, using an electric hand whisk, beat together until just smooth. Spoon the mixture into the paper cases.

3 Bake the cupcakes in a preheated oven, 180°C/350°F/ Gas Mark 4, for 15–20 minutes or until well risen, golden brown and firm to the touch. Transfer to a wire rack to cool.

4 To make the topping, put the butter in a bowl and beat until fluffy. Sift in the icing sugar and beat together until smooth and creamy. When the cupcakes are cold, spread a little frosting on top of each cupcake, then decorate to your choice and, if desired, place a candle in the top of each.

gold & silver anniversary cupcakes

ingredients

makes 24

225 g/8 oz butter, softened
225 g/8 oz caster sugar
1 tsp vanilla essence
4 large eggs, lightly beaten
225 g/8 oz self-raising flour
5 tbsp milk

topping

175 g/6 oz unsalted butter
350 g/12 oz icing sugar
silver or gold dragées
   (cake decoration balls)

method

1 Put 24 silver or gold foil cake cases in muffin pans, or arrange them on baking sheets.

2 Put the butter, sugar and vanilla essence in a bowl and beat together until light and fluffy. Gradually add the eggs, beating well after each addition. Add the flour and, using a large metal spoon, fold into the mixture with the milk. Spoon the mixture into the paper cases.

3 Bake the cupcakes in a preheated oven, 180°C/350°F/Gas Mark 4, for 15–20 minutes or until well risen and firm to the touch. Transfer to a wire rack to cool.

4 To make the topping, put the butter in a large bowl and beat until fluffy. Sift in the icing sugar and beat together until well mixed. Put the topping in a piping bag fitted with a medium star-shaped nozzle.

5 When the cupcakes are cold, pipe icing on top of each. Sprinkle over the silver or gold dragées before serving.

lavender fairy cakes

ingredients

makes 12

115 g/4 oz golden caster sugar
115 g/4 oz butter, softened
2 eggs, beaten
1 tbsp milk
1 tsp finely chopped lavender
    flowers
½ tsp vanilla essence
175 g/6 oz self-raising flour, sifted
150 g/5½ oz icing sugar

to decorate
lavender flowers
silver dragées

method

1 Place 12 paper cake cases in a muffin pan. Place the caster sugar and butter in a bowl and cream together until pale and fluffy. Gradually beat in the eggs. Stir in the milk, lavender and vanilla essence, then carefully fold in the flour.

2 Divide the mixture between the paper cases and bake in a preheated oven, 200°C/400°F/Gas Mark 6, for 12–15 minutes or until well risen and golden. The sponge should bounce back when pressed.

3 A few minutes before the cakes are ready, sift the icing sugar into a bowl and stir in enough water to make a thick icing.

4 When the fairy cakes are baked, transfer to a wire rack and place a blob of icing in the centre of each one, allowing it to run across the cake. Decorate with lavender flowers and silver dragées and serve as soon as the cakes are cool.

iced cupcakes

ingredients

makes 12

115 g/4 oz butter, softened
115 g/4 oz caster sugar
2 eggs, lightly beaten
115 g/4 oz self-raising flour

topping

200 g/7 oz icing sugar
about 2 tbsp warm water
a few drops of food colouring
   (optional)
sugar flowers, hundreds and
   thousands, glacé cherries,
   and/or chocolate strands,
   to decorate

method

1 Line two 12-hole muffin pans with 16 paper cases.
   Place the butter and sugar in a large bowl and beat
   together until light and fluffy, then gradually beat in
   the eggs. Sift in the flour and fold into the mixture.
   Spoon the mixture into the paper cases.

2 Bake in a preheated oven, 190°C/375°F/Gas Mark 5,
   for 15–20 minutes. Transfer to a wire rack to cool
   completely.

3 To make the topping, sift the icing sugar into a bowl
   and stir in just enough warm water to mix to a smooth
   paste that is thick enough to coat the back of a
   wooden spoon. Stir in a few drops of food colouring,
   if using, then spread the topping over the cupcakes
   and decorate, as liked.

boutique cupcakes

ingredients

makes 10

175 g/6 oz butter, softened,
    or soft margarine
175 g/6 oz caster sugar
1 tsp vanilla extract
3 eggs, lightly beaten
150 g/5 oz raspberries
225 g/8 oz self-raising flour

topping

225 g/8 oz butter, softened
1 tbsp cream or milk
350 g/12 oz icing sugar

for decorating

pink, black, red and yellow
    food colouring
3 oz/85 g ready-to-roll fondant
    icing
silver dragées
jelly sweets

method

1 Line a 12-hole muffin pan with 10 paper cases. Place the butter and sugar in a large bowl and beat together until light and fluffy, then beat in the vanilla extract. Gradually beat in the eggs, then fold the raspberries and flour into the mixture. Spoon the mixture into the paper cases.

2 Bake in a preheated oven, 350°C/180°F/Gas Mark 4, for 20–25 minutes, or until golden brown and springy to the touch. Transfer to a wire rack to cool completely.

3 To make the topping, place the butter and cream in a bowl and beat together. Gradually sift in the icing sugar and beat until smooth.

4 To decorate, colour the topping pale pink, then place in a pastry bag fitted with a large star nozzle and pipe the topping on top of the cakes.

5 Colour the fondant icing and then mould into different shapes, such as handbags, high-heeled shoes or rings. Arrange the shapes on the cupcakes, then press silver dragées into the icing to form the handle of the bag and to decorate the shoes. Use jelly sweets to make the gems on the rings.

rose petal muffins

ingredients

makes 12

1 tbsp sunflower or peanut oil, for oiling (if using)
225 g/8 oz plain flour
2 tsp baking powder
pinch of salt
4 tbsp butter
6 tbsp caster sugar
1 large egg, beaten
110 ml/4 fl oz milk
1 tsp rose water
50 g/1¾ oz edible rose petals, rinsed, patted dry and lightly snipped

topping

100 g/3½ oz icing sugar
1 tbsp liquid glucose
1 tbsp rose water
50 g/1¾ oz edible rose petals, rinsed and patted dry

method

1 Oil a 12-cup muffin pan with sunflower oil, or line it with 12 muffin paper cases. Sift the flour, baking powder and salt into a large mixing bowl.

2 In a separate large bowl, cream together the butter and caster sugar, then stir in the beaten egg, milk, rose water and snipped rose petals. Add the butter mixture to the flour mixture and then gently stir together until just combined. Do not overstir the mixture – it is fine for it to be a little lumpy.

3 Divide the muffin mixture evenly between the 12 cups in the muffin pan or the paper cases (they should be about two-thirds full). Transfer to a preheated oven, 200°C/400°F/Gas Mark 6, and bake for 20 minutes or until risen and golden.

4 While the muffins are cooking, make the topping. Place the icing sugar in a bowl, then stir in the liquid glucose and rose water. Cover with clingfilm until ready to use.

5 When the muffins are cooked, remove them from the oven and place on a wire rack to cool. When they have cooled, spread each muffin with some of the topping, strew over and/or around with the rose petals and serve.

rose-topped wedding muffins

ingredients

makes 12

280 g/10 oz plain flour
1 tbsp baking powder
pinch of salt
115 g/4 oz caster sugar
2 eggs
250 ml/9 fl oz milk
6 tbsp sunflower oil or 85 g/3 oz
    butter, melted and cooled
1 tsp vanilla extract

topping

175 g/6 oz icing sugar
3–4 tsp hot water
12 ready-made sugar roses,
    to decorate

method

1 Increase the quantity of ingredients according to the number of wedding guests invited; double quantities each time to make 24 muffins. Line the appropriate number of muffin pans with paper liners.

2 Sift together the flour, baking powder and salt into a large bowl. Stir in the sugar. Place the eggs in a large jug or bowl and beat lightly, then beat in the milk, oil and vanilla extract. Make a well in the centre of the dry ingredients and pour in the beaten liquid ingredients. Stir gently until just combined; do not overmix. Spoon the mixture into the paper cases.

3 Bake in a preheated oven, 400°F/200°C/Gas Mark 6, for 20 minutes, or until well risen, golden brown and firm to the touch. Leave to cool in the pan or pans for 5 minutes, then transfer to a wire rack to cool completely. Store in the freezer until required.

4 For the topping, sift the icing sugar into a bowl. Add the water and stir until the mixture is smooth and thick enough to coat the back of a wooden spoon. Spoon the icing on top of each muffin, then top with a sugar rose.

mother's day breakfast muffins

ingredients

makes 12

280 g/10 oz plain flour
1 tbsp baking powder
pinch of salt
115 g/4 oz caster sugar
2 eggs
250 ml/9 fl oz milk
6 tbsp sunflower oil or 85 g/3 oz
    butter, melted and cooled
1 tsp orange extract
fresh strawberries, for serving
icing sugar, for dusting

method

1 Line a 12-hole muffin pan with 12 paper cases. Sift together the flour, baking powder and salt into a large bowl. Stir in the caster sugar.

2 Place the eggs in a large jug or bowl and beat lightly, then beat in the milk, oil and orange extract. Make a well in the centre of the dry ingredients and pour in the beaten liquid ingredients. Stir gently until just combined; do not overmix. Spoon the batter into the paper cases.

3 Bake in a preheated oven, 200°C/400°F/Gas Mark 6, for 20 minutes, or until well risen, golden brown and firm to the touch. Let cool in the pan for 5 minutes. Meanwhile, arrange the strawberries in a bowl. Dust the muffins with sifted icing sugar and serve warm.

children's party muffins

ingredients
makes 12

280 g/10 oz plain flour
1 tbsp baking powder
½ tsp salt
115 g/4 oz caster sugar
2 eggs
250 ml/9 fl oz milk
6 tbsp sunflower oil or 85 g/3 oz
   butter, melted and cooled
1 tsp vanilla extract

topping
175 g/6 oz icing sugar
3–4 tsp hot water
variety of small sweets, to decorate

method

1 Line a 12-hole muffin pan with 12 paper cases. Sift together the flour, baking powder, and salt into a large bowl. Stir in the caster sugar.

2 Place the eggs in a large jug or bowl and beat lightly, then beat in the milk, oil and vanilla extract. Make a well in the centre of the dry ingredients and pour in the beaten liquid ingredients. Stir until combined. Spoon the mixture into the paper cases.

3 Bake in a preheated oven, 200°C/400°F/Gas Mark 6, for 20 minutes, or until well risen, golden brown and firm to the touch. Leave to cool in the pan for 5 minutes, then transfer to a wire rack to cool completely.

4 When the muffins are cold, make the topping. Sift the icing sugar into a bowl. Add the water and stir until the mixture is smooth and thick enough to coat the back of a wooden spoon. Spoon the icing on top of each muffin, then add the decoration of your choice. Leave to set for about 30 minutes before serving.

mocha muffins

ingredients

makes 12

1 tbsp sunflower or peanut oil,
    for oiling (if using)
225 g/8 oz plain flour
1 tbsp baking powder
2 tbsp cocoa powder
pinch of salt
115 g/4 oz butter, melted
150 g/5½ oz raw sugar
1 large egg, beaten
110 ml/4 fl oz milk
1 tsp almond essence
2 tbsp strong coffee
1 tbsp instant coffee powder
55 g/2 oz plain chocolate chips
25 g/1 oz raisins

topping

3 tbsp raw sugar
1 tbsp cocoa powder
1 tsp allspice

method

1 Oil a 12-cup muffin pan with sunflower oil, or line it with 12 muffin paper cases. Sift the flour, baking powder, cocoa and salt into a large mixing bowl.

2 In a separate large bowl, cream the butter and raw sugar together, then stir in the beaten egg. Pour in the milk, almond essence and coffee, then add the coffee powder, chocolate chips and raisins and gently mix together. Add the raisin mixture to the flour mixture and stir together until just combined. Do not overstir the mixture – it is fine for it to be a little lumpy.

3 Divide the muffin mixture evenly between the 12 cups in the muffin pan or the paper cases (they should be about two-thirds full). To make the topping, place the raw sugar in a bowl, add the cocoa and allspice and mix together well.

4 Sprinkle the topping over the muffins, then transfer to a preheated oven, 190°C/375°F/Gas Mark 5, and bake for 20 minutes or until risen and golden. Remove the muffins from the oven and serve warm, or place them on a wire rack to cool.

marshmallow muffins

ingredients

makes 12

70 g/2½ oz butter
275 g/10 oz plain flour
6 tbsp cocoa powder
3 tsp baking powder
85 g/3 oz caster sugar
100 g/3½ oz milk chocolate chips
55 g/2 oz multicoloured mini
  marshmallows
1 large egg, beaten
300 ml/10 fl oz milk

method

1 Line a 12-cup muffin pan with muffin paper cases.
  Melt the butter in a pan.

2 Sift the flour, cocoa and baking powder together into
  a large bowl. Stir in the sugar, chocolate chips and
  marshmallows until thoroughly mixed.

3 Whisk the egg, milk and melted butter together in a
  separate bowl, then gently stir into the flour to form
  a stiff mixture. Divide the mixture evenly between the
  muffin liners.

4 Bake in a preheated oven, 190°C/375°F/Gas Mark 5,
  for 20–25 minutes or until well risen and golden
  brown. Remove from the oven and cool in the pan
  for 5 minutes, then place on a wire rack to cool
  completely.

christmas snowflake muffins

ingredients

makes 12

280 g/10 oz plain flour
1 tbsp baking powder
1 tsp allspice
pinch of salt
115 g/4 oz soft dark brown sugar
2 eggs
100 ml/3½ fl oz milk
6 tbsp sunflower oil or 85 g/3 oz
   butter, melted and cooled
⅔ cup mixed dried fruit with
   cherries and nuts

topping

1 lb/450 g ready-to-roll
   fondant icing
icing sugar, for dusting
2½ tsp apricot jam
silver dragées, to decorate

method

1 Line a 12-hole muffin pan with 12 paper cases. Sift together the flour, baking powder, allspice and salt into a large bowl. Stir in the brown sugar.

2 Place the eggs in a large jug or bowl and beat lightly, then beat in the milk and oil. Make a well in the centre of the dry ingredients and pour in the liquid ingredients and dried fruit. Stir until combined; do not overmix. Spoon the mixture into the paper cases.

3 Bake in a preheated oven, 200°C/400°F/Gas Mark 6, for 20 minutes, or until well risen, golden brown and firm to the touch. Leave to cool in the pan for 5 minutes, then transfer to a wire rack and leave to cool completely.

4 Knead the fondant until pliable. Roll out the fondant on a surface dusted with icing sugar to a thickness of 5 mm/¼ inch. Using a 7-cm/2¾-inch fluted cutter, cut out 12 'snowflakes'.

5 Heat the apricot jam until runny, then brush over the tops of the muffins. Place a snowflake on top of each one, then decorate with silver dragées.

brandied cherry muffins

ingredients

makes 12

1 tbsp sunflower or peanut oil,
   for oiling (if using)
225 g/8 oz plain flour
1 tbsp baking powder
pinch of salt
3 tbsp butter
2 tbsp caster sugar
1 large egg, beaten
200 ml/7 fl oz milk
2 tsp cherry brandy
300 g/10½ oz drained canned
   cherries, chopped

method

1 Oil a 12-cup muffin pan with sunflower oil, or line it with 12 muffin paper cases. Sift the flour, baking powder and salt into a large mixing bowl.

2 In a separate large bowl, cream the butter and caster sugar together, then stir in the beaten egg. Pour in the milk and cherry brandy, then add the chopped cherries and gently stir together. Add the cherry mixture to the flour mixture, then gently stir together until just combined. Do not overstir the mixture – it is fine for it to be a little lumpy.

3 Divide the muffin mixture between the 12 cups in the muffin pan or the paper cases (they should be about two-thirds full). Transfer to a preheated oven, 200°C/400°F/Gas Mark 6, and bake for 20–25 minutes or until risen and golden. Remove from the oven and serve warm, or place them on a wire rack to cool.

apricot muffins with cointreau

ingredients

makes 12

1 tbsp sunflower or peanut oil,
    for oiling (if using)
125 g/4½ oz self-raising flour
2 tsp baking powder
175 g/6 oz butter
125 g/4½ oz caster sugar
2 large eggs, beaten
110 ml/4 fl oz milk
4 tbsp single cream
1 tbsp orange-flavoured liqueur,
    such as Cointreau
85 g/3 oz no-soak dried
    apricots, chopped
85 g/3 oz no-soak dried dates,
    pitted and chopped

topping

3 tbsp raw sugar
1 tsp ground cinnamon
1 tbsp freshly grated
    orange rind

method

1 Oil a 12-cup muffin pan with sunflower oil, or line it
    with 12 muffin paper cases.

2 Sift the flour and baking powder into a large mixing
    bowl.

3 In a separate large bowl, cream together the butter
    and caster sugar, then stir in the beaten eggs. Pour in
    the milk, cream and orange-flavoured liqueur, then
    add the chopped apricots and dates and gently mix
    together. Add the fruit mixture to the flour mixture and
    then gently stir together until just combined. Do not
    overstir the mixture – it is fine for it to be a little lumpy.

4 Divide the muffin mixture evenly between the 12 cups
    in the muffin pan or the paper cases (they should be
    about two-thirds full). To make the topping, place the
    raw sugar in a small bowl, then mix in the cinnamon
    and orange rind. Sprinkle the topping over the muffins,
    then transfer to the oven and bake in a preheated
    oven, 190°C/375°F/Gas Mark 5, for 20 minutes or until
    risen and golden. Remove the muffins from the oven
    and serve warm, or place them on a wire rack to cool.

vanilla hearts

ingredients

makes 12

225 g/8 oz plain flour, plus extra
for dusting
150 g/5½ oz butter, cut into small
pieces, plus extra for greasing
125 g/4½ oz caster sugar, plus
extra for dusting
1 tsp vanilla essence

method

1 Sift the flour into a large bowl. Add the butter and rub
it in with your fingertips until the mixture resembles
fine breadcrumbs. Stir in the caster sugar and vanilla
essence and mix together to form a firm dough.

2 Roll out the dough on a lightly floured work surface to
a thickness of 2.5 cm/1 inch. Stamp out 12 hearts with
a heart-shaped biscuit cutter measuring 5 cm/2 inches
across and 2.5 cm/1 inch deep. Arrange the hearts on
a lightly greased baking sheet.

3 Bake in a preheated oven, 180°C/350°F/Gas Mark 4, for
15–20 minutes or until the hearts are a light golden
colour. Transfer the vanilla hearts to a wire rack to cool
completely. Dust them with a little caster sugar just
before serving.

simply
delicious

sweet shop vanilla cupcakes

ingredients
makes 18

140 g/5 oz butter, softened,
    or soft margarine
140 g/5 oz caster sugar
1½ tsp vanilla extract
2 large eggs, lightly beaten
200 g/7 oz self-raising flour

topping
225 g/8 oz butter, softened
1 tbsp cream or milk
350 g/12 oz icing sugar
a selection of classic small sweets,
    such as jelly beans,
    to decorate

method

1 Line two 12-hole muffin pans with 18 paper cases.

2 Place the butter and sugar in a large bowl and beat together until light and fluffy, then beat in the vanilla extract. Gradually beat in the eggs, then sift in the flour and fold into the mixture. Spoon the batter into the paper cases.

3 Bake in a preheated oven, 190°C/375°F/Gas Mark 5, for 12–15 minutes, or until golden and springy to the touch. Transfer to a wire rack to cool completely.

4 To make the topping, place the butter and milk in a bowl and beat together. Gradually sift in the icing sugar and beat until smooth.

5 Place the buttercream in a pastry bag fitted with a small star nozzle and pipe the buttercream on top of each cake. Arrange the sweets on top to decorate.

drizzled honey cupcakes

ingredients

makes 12

85 g/3 oz self-raising flour
¼ tsp ground cinnamon
pinch of ground cloves
pinch of grated nutmeg
6 tbsp butter, softened
85 g/3 oz caster sugar
1 tbsp honey
finely grated rind of 1 orange
2 eggs, lightly beaten
40 g/1½ oz walnut pieces,
    finely chopped

topping

15 g/½ oz walnut pieces,
    finely chopped
¼ tsp ground cinnamon
2 tbsp honey
juice of 1 orange

method

1 Put 12 paper baking cases in a muffin pan, or place 12 double-layer paper cases on a baking sheet.

2 Sift the flour, cinnamon, cloves and nutmeg together into a bowl. Put the butter and sugar in a separate bowl and beat together until light and fluffy. Beat in the honey and orange rind, then gradually add the eggs, beating well after each addition. Using a metal spoon, fold in the flour mixture. Stir in the walnuts, then spoon the mixture into the paper cases.

3 Bake the cupcakes in a preheated oven, 190°C/375°F/ Gas Mark 5, for 20 minutes or until well risen and golden brown. Transfer to a wire rack to cool.

4 To make the topping, mix together the walnuts and cinnamon. Put the honey and orange juice in a pan and heat gently, stirring, until combined.

5 When the cupcakes have almost cooled, prick the tops all over with a fork or skewer and then drizzle with the warm honey mixture. Sprinkle a little of the walnut mixture over the top of each cupcake and serve warm or cold.

sticky gingerbread cupcakes

ingredients

makes 16

115 g/4 oz plain flour
2 tsp ground ginger
¾ tsp ground cinnamon
1 piece of preserved
    ginger, finely chopped
¾ tsp bicarbonate of soda
4 tbsp milk
6 tbsp butter, softened,
    or soft margarine
70 g/2½ oz brown sugar
2 tbsp molasses
2 eggs, lightly beaten
pieces of preserved ginger,
    to decorate

topping

6 tbsp butter, softened
175 g/6 oz icing sugar
2 tbsp ginger syrup from the
    preserved ginger jar

method

1 Put 16 paper baking cases in a muffin pan, or place
   16 double-layer paper cases on a baking sheet.

2 Sift the flour, ground ginger and cinnamon together
   into a bowl. Add the finely chopped ginger and toss in
   the flour mixture until well coated. In a separate bowl,
   dissolve the bicarbonate of soda in the milk.

3 Put the butter and sugar in a bowl and beat together
   until fluffy. Beat in the molasses, then gradually add
   the eggs, beating well after each addition. Beat in the
   flour mixture, then gradually beat in the milk. Spoon
   the mixture into the paper cases.

4 Bake the cupcakes in a preheated oven, 160°C/325°F/
   Gas Mark 3, for 20 minutes or until well risen and
   golden brown. Transfer to a wire rack to cool.

5 To make the frosting, put the butter in a bowl and beat
   until fluffy. Sift in the sugar, add the ginger syrup and
   beat together until smooth and creamy. Slice the
   preserved ginger into thin slivers or chop finely.

6 When the cupcakes are cold, spread a little frosting
   on top of each cupcake, then decorate with pieces
   of ginger.

marbled chocolate cupcakes

ingredients

makes 21

175 g/6 oz soft margarine
175 g/6 oz caster sugar
3 eggs
175 g/6 oz self-raising flour
2 tbsp milk
55 g/2 oz plain chocolate,
    melted

method

1 Put 21 paper baking cases in a muffin pan, or place
   21 double-layer paper cases on a baking sheet.

2 Put the margarine, sugar, eggs, flour and milk in a large
   bowl and, using an electric hand whisk, beat together
   until just smooth.

3 Divide the mixture between 2 bowls. Add the melted
   chocolate to one bowl and stir together until well
   mixed. Using a teaspoon, and alternating the chocolate
   mixture with the plain mixture, put four half-teaspoons
   into each paper case.

4 Bake the cupcakes in a preheated oven, 180°C/350°F/
   Gas Mark 4, for 20 minutes or until well risen and
   springy to the touch. Transfer to a wire rack to cool.

variation

Add the grated rind and juice of ½ small orange and
a few drops of orange food colouring to the plain
cake mixture.

carrot cake

ingredients

makes 6

butter, for greasing
115 g/4 oz self-raising flour
pinch of salt
1 tsp ground allspice
½ tsp ground nutmeg
175 g/6 oz soft brown sugar
2 eggs, beaten
5 tbsp sunflower oil
175 g/6 oz grated carrots
1 banana, chopped
25 g/1 oz chopped toasted
    mixed nuts

topping

3 tbsp butter, softened
3 tbsp cream cheese
175 g/6 oz icing sugar, sifted
1 tsp orange juice
grated rind of ½ orange
walnut halves or pieces,
    to decorate

method

1 Grease an 18-cm/7-inch square cake tin with butter and line with baking parchment. Sift the flour, salt, allspice and nutmeg into a bowl. Stir in the brown sugar, then stir in the eggs and oil. Add the carrots, banana and chopped mixed nuts and mix the ingredients together well.

2 Spoon the mixture into the prepared cake tin and level the surface. Transfer to a preheated oven, 190°C/375°F/ Gas Mark 5, and bake for 55 minutes or until golden and just firm to the touch. Remove from the oven and cool. When cool enough to handle, turn out on to a wire rack to cool completely.

3 To make the frosting, put the butter, cream cheese, icing sugar, orange juice and orange rind into a bowl and beat together until creamy. Spread the frosting over the top of the cold cake, then use a fork to make shallow wavy lines in the frosting. Scatter over the walnuts, cut the cake into bars and serve.

queen cakes

ingredients

makes 18

8 tbsp butter, softened,
    or soft margarine
115 g/4 oz caster sugar
2 large eggs, lightly beaten
4 tsp lemon juice
175 g/6 oz self-raising flour
115 g/4 oz currants
2–4 tbsp milk, if necessary

method

1 Put 18 paper baking cases in a muffin pan, or place
   18 double-layer paper cases on a baking sheet.

2 Put the butter and sugar in a bowl and beat together
   until light and fluffy. Gradually beat in the eggs, then
   beat in the lemon juice with 1 tablespoon of the flour.
   Using a metal spoon, fold in the remaining flour and
   the currants, adding a little milk if necessary, to give
   a soft dropping consistency. Spoon the mixture into
   the paper cases.

3 Bake the cupcakes in a preheated oven, 190°C/375°F/
   Gas Mark 5, for 15–20 minutes or until well risen and
   golden brown. Transfer to a wire rack to cool.

doughnut muffins

ingredients

makes 12

175 g/6 oz butter, softened,
   plus extra for greasing
200 g/7 oz caster sugar
2 large eggs, lightly beaten
375 g/13 oz plain flour
¾ tbsp baking powder
¼ tsp bicarbonate of soda
pinch of salt
½ tsp freshly grated nutmeg
250 ml/9 fl oz milk

topping

100 g/3½ oz caster sugar
1 tsp ground cinnamon
2 tbsp butter, melted

method

1 Grease a deep 12-cup muffin pan. In a large bowl, beat the butter and sugar together until light and creamy. Add the eggs, a little at a time, beating well between additions.

2 Sift the flour, baking powder, bicarbonate of soda, salt and nutmeg together. Add half to the creamed mixture with half of the milk. Gently fold together the ingredients before incorporating the remaining flour and milk. Spoon the mixture into the prepared muffin pan, filling each hole to about two-thirds full.

3 Bake in a preheated oven, 180°C/350°F/Gas Mark 4, for 15–20 minutes or until the muffins are lightly brown and firm to the touch.

4 For the topping, mix the sugar and cinnamon together. While the muffins are still warm from the oven, brush lightly with melted butter, and sprinkle over the cinnamon and sugar mixture. Eat warm or cold.

lime & poppy seed muffins

ingredients

makes 12

175 ml/6 fl oz sunflower
    or peanut oil, plus extra
    for oiling (if using)
225 g/8 oz plain flour
1 tsp baking powder
½ tsp salt
225 g/8 oz caster sugar
1 large egg
1 large egg white
150 ml/5 fl oz milk
1 tbsp lime juice
1 tbsp grated lime rind
2 tsp poppy seeds

to decorate
2 tsp grated lime rind
1–2 tsp poppy seeds

method

1 Oil a 12-cup muffin pan with sunflower oil, or line it
   with 12 muffin paper cases.

2 Sift the flour, baking powder and salt into a mixing
   bowl. Then add the caster sugar and stir together.

3 In a separate bowl, whisk the egg, egg white,
   remaining sunflower oil and milk together, then stir
   in the lime juice and grated lime rind. Add the egg
   mixture to the flour mixture, then add the poppy
   seeds and gently stir. Do not overstir the mixture –
   it is fine for it to be a little lumpy.

4 Divide the muffin mixture evenly between the 12 cups
   in the muffin pan or the paper cases (they should be
   about two-thirds full). Sprinkle over the grated lime
   rind and poppy seeds to decorate, then bake in a
   preheated oven, 190°C/375°F/Gas Mark 5, for 25
   minutes or until risen and golden. Serve the muffins
   warm, or place them on a wire rack to cool.

buttermilk scones

ingredients

makes 8

300 g/10½ oz self-raising flour,
    plus extra for dusting
1 tsp baking powder
pinch of salt
55 g/2 oz cold butter, cut into
    pieces, plus extra for greasing
40 g/1½ oz golden caster sugar
300 ml/10 fl oz buttermilk
2 tbsp milk
whipped cream and strawberry
    jam, to serve

method

1 Sift the flour, baking powder and salt into a bowl. Add the butter and rub in until the mixture resembles fine breadcrumbs. Add the sugar and buttermilk and quickly mix together.

2 Turn the mixture out onto a floured work surface and knead lightly. Roll out to 2.5-cm/1-inch thick. Using a 6-cm/2½-inch plain or fluted cutter, stamp out the scones and place on a greased baking sheet. Gather the trimmings, re-roll and stamp out more scones until all the dough is used up.

3 Brush the tops of the scones with milk. Bake in a preheated oven, 220°C/425°F/Gas Mark 7, for 12–15 minutes or until well risen and golden. Transfer to a wire rack to cool. Split and serve with whipped cream and strawberry jam.

petticoat tail shortbread

ingredients

makes 8

175 g/6 oz plain flour, plus
    1 tbsp for dusting
pinch of salt
55 g/2 oz caster sugar
115 g/4 oz butter, cut into small
    pieces, plus extra for greasing
2 tsp golden caster sugar

method

1 Mix together the flour, salt and sugar. Rub the butter
  into the dry ingredients. Continue to work the mixture
  until it forms a soft dough. Make sure you do not
  overwork the dough or the shortbread will be tough,
  not crumbly as it should be.

2 Lightly press the dough into a greased 20-cm/8-inch
  fluted cake tin. Alternatively, roll out the dough on a
  lightly floured work surface, place on a baking sheet
  and pinch the edges to form a scalloped pattern.

3 Mark into 8 pieces with a knife. Prick the shortbread all
  over with a fork and bake in the centre of a preheated
  oven, 150°C/300°F/Gas Mark 2, for 45–50 minutes until
  the shortbread is firm and just coloured.

4 Cool in the tin and dredge with the sugar. Cut into
  portions and remove to a wire rack. Store in an airtight
  container in a cool place until needed.

rock drops

ingredients

makes 8

100 g/3½ oz butter, cut into small
    pieces, plus extra for greasing
200 g/7 oz plain flour
2 tsp baking powder
75 g/2¾ oz golden caster sugar
100 g/3½ oz sultanas
25 g/1 oz glacé cherries,
    finely chopped
1 egg, beaten
2 tbsp milk

method

1 Lightly grease a baking sheet, large enough for 8 big
    rock drops, with a little butter.

2 Sift the flour and baking powder into a mixing bowl.
    Rub in the butter with your fingertips until the mixture
    resembles fine breadcrumbs. Stir in the sugar, sultanas
    and chopped glacé cherries, mixing well. Add the
    beaten egg and the milk to the mixture and mix to
    form a soft dough.

3 Spoon 8 mounds of the mixture onto the prepared
    baking sheet, spacing them well apart as they will
    spread while cooking. Bake in a preheated oven,
    200°C/400°F/Gas Mark 6, for 15–20 minutes or until
    firm to the touch.

4 Remove the rock drops from the baking sheet. Either
    serve immediately or transfer to a wire rack to cool
    before serving.

healthy options

banana muffins with cinnamon frosting

ingredients

makes 12

150 g/5½oz gluten-free plain flour
1 tsp gluten-free baking powder
pinch of salt
150 g/5½oz caster sugar
6 tbsp dairy-free milk
2 eggs, lightly beaten
150 g/5½oz dairy-free
    margarine, melted
2 small bananas, mashed

frosting

50 g/1¾oz vegan cream cheese
2 tbsp dairy-free margarine
¼ tsp ground cinnamon
90 g/3¼oz icing sugar

method

1 Place 12 large paper cases in a deep muffin pan. Sift the flour, baking powder and salt together into a mixing bowl. Stir in the sugar.

2 Whisk the milk, eggs and margarine together in a separate bowl until combined. Slowly stir into the flour mixture without beating. Fold in the mashed bananas.

3 Spoon the mixture into the paper cases and bake in a preheated oven, 200°C/400°F/Gas Mark 6, for 20 minutes or until risen and golden. Turn out onto a wire rack to cool.

4 To make the frosting, beat the cream cheese and margarine together in a bowl, then beat in the cinnamon and icing sugar until smooth and creamy. Chill the frosting in the refrigerator for about 15 minutes to firm up, then top each muffin with a spoonful.

banana & date muffins

ingredients

makes 12

vegetable oil cooking spray,
    for oiling (if using)
225 g/8 oz plain flour
2 tsp baking powder
¼ tsp salt
½ tsp allspice
5 tbsp caster sugar
2 large egg whites
2 ripe bananas, sliced
55 g/2 oz no-soak dried dates,
    pitted and chopped
4 tbsp skimmed milk
5 tbsp maple syrup

method

1 Spray a 12-cup muffin pan with vegetable oil cooking spray, or line it with 12 muffin paper cases. Sift the flour, baking powder, salt and allspice into a mixing bowl. Add the caster sugar and mix together.

2 In a separate bowl, whisk the egg whites together. Mash the sliced bananas in a separate bowl, then add them to the egg whites. Add the dates, then pour in the milk and maple syrup and stir together gently to mix. Add the banana and date mixture to the flour mixture and then gently stir together until just combined. Do not overstir the mixture – it is fine for it to be a little lumpy.

3 Divide the muffin mixture evenly between the 12 cups in the muffin pan or the paper cases (they should be about two-thirds full). Bake in a preheated oven, 200°C/400°F/Gas Mark 6, for 25 minutes or until risen and golden. Remove the muffins from the oven and serve warm, or place them on a wire rack to cool.

wheatgerm, banana & pumpkin seed muffins

ingredients

makes 12

6 tbsp sunflower oil, plus extra
    for greasing
140 g/5 oz plain flour
1 tbsp baking powder
115 g/4 oz caster sugar
140 g/5 oz wheatgerm
85 g/3 oz pumpkin seeds
2 bananas
about 150 ml/5 fl oz
    skimmed milk
2 eggs

method

1 Grease a 12-hole muffin pan. Sift together the flour and baking powder into a large bowl. Stir in the sugar, wheatgerm and 50 g/1¾ oz of the pumpkin seeds. Mash the bananas and place in a jug, then add enough milk to make up the purée to 250 ml/9 fl oz.

2 Place the eggs in a large jug or bowl and beat lightly, then beat in the banana and milk mixture and the oil. Make a well in the centre of the dry ingredients and pour in the beaten liquid ingredients. Stir gently until just combined; do not overmix. Spoon the mixture into the muffin pan. Sprinkle the remaining pumpkin seeds over the top.

3 Bake in a preheated oven, 200°C/400°F/Gas Mark 6, for 20 minutes, or until well risen, golden brown and firm to the touch. Leave the muffins to cool in the tin for 5 minutes, then serve warm or transfer to a wire rack to cool completely.

muesli muffins

ingredients

makes 12

140 g/5 oz plain flour
1 tbsp baking powder
280 g/10 oz unsweetened muesli
115 g/4 oz soft light brown sugar
2 eggs
250 ml/9 fl oz buttermilk
6 tbsp sunflower oil

method

1 Line a 12-hole muffin pan with 12 paper cases. Sift together the flour and baking powder into a large bowl. Stir in the muesli and sugar.

2 Place the eggs in a large jug or bowl and beat lightly, then beat in the buttermilk and oil. Make a well in the centre of the dry ingredients and pour in the beaten liquid ingredients. Stir gently until just combined; do not overmix. Spoon the mixture into the paper cases.

3 Bake in a preheated oven, 200°C/400°F/Gas Mark 6, for 20 minutes, or until well risen, golden brown and firm to the touch. Leave to cool in the tin for 5 minutes, then serve warm or transfer to a wire rack to cool completely.

yogurt & spice muffins

ingredients

makes 12

140 g/5 oz wholemeal flour
140 g/5 oz plain flour
1 tbsp baking powder
½ tsp bicarbonate of soda
4 tsp mixed spice
115 g/4 oz caster sugar
100 g/3½ oz mixed dried fruit
2 eggs
250 ml/9 fl oz low-fat
    natural yogurt
6 tbsp sunflower oil

method

1 Line a 12-hole muffin pan with 12 paper cases. Sift together both types of flour, the baking powder, baking soda and mixed spice into a large bowl, adding any bran left in the sieve. Stir in the sugar and dried fruit.

2 Place the eggs in a large jug or bowl and beat lightly, then beat in the yogurt and oil. Make a well in the centre of the dry ingredients and pour in the beaten liquid ingredients. Stir gently until just combined; do not overmix. Spoon the mixture into the paper cases.

3 Bake in a preheated oven, 200°C/400°F/Gas Mark 6, for 20 minutes, or until well risen, golden brown and firm to the touch. Leave to cool in the tin for 5 minutes, then serve warm or transfer to a wire rack to cool completely.

three grain muffins

ingredients

makes 12

6 tbsp sunflower oil, plus
    extra for greasing
75 g/2¾ oz wholemeal flour
75 g/2¾ oz plain flour
1 tbsp baking powder
115 g/4 oz soft dark brown sugar
60 g/2¼ oz medium polenta
70 g/2½ oz porridge oats
2 eggs
250 ml/9 fl oz buttermilk
1 tsp vanilla extract

method

1 Grease a 12-hole muffin pan. Sift together the flours and the baking powder into a large bowl, adding any bran left in the sieve. Stir in the sugar, polenta and oats.

2 Place the eggs in a large jug or bowl and beat lightly, then beat in the buttermilk, oil and vanilla extract. Make a well in the centre of the dry ingredients and pour in the beaten liquid ingredients. Stir gently until just combined; do not overmix. Spoon the mixture into the muffin pan.

3 Bake in a preheated oven, 200°C/400°F/Gas Mark 6, for 20 minutes, or until well risen, golden brown and firm to the touch. Leave the muffins to cool in the tin for 5 minutes, then serve warm or transfer to a wire rack to cool completely.

apple & raspberry muffins

ingredients

makes 12

3 large baking apples,
   peeled and cored
450 ml/16 fl oz water
1½ tsp allspice
vegetable oil cooking spray,
   for oiling (if using)
300 g/10½ oz plain
   wholewheat flour
1 tbsp baking powder
¼ tsp salt
3 tbsp caster sugar
85 g/3 oz fresh raspberries

method

1 Thinly slice 2 baking apples and place them in a
   saucepan with 6 tablespoons of the water. Bring to the
   boil, then reduce the heat. Stir in ½ teaspoon of the
   allspice, cover the pan and simmer, stirring occasionally,
   for 15–20 minutes or until the water has been
   absorbed. Remove from the heat and cool. Blend in
   a food processor until smooth. Stir in the remaining
   water and mix well.

2 Spray a 12-cup muffin pan with vegetable oil cooking
   spray, or line it with 12 muffin paper cases. Sift the
   flour, baking powder, salt and remaining allspice into
   a mixing bowl. Then stir in the sugar.

3 Chop the remaining apple and add to the flour
   mixture. Add the raspberries, then combine gently
   with the flour mixture until lightly coated. Finally,
   gently stir in the cooled apple/water mixture. Do not
   overstir the mixture – it is fine for it to be a little lumpy.

4 Divide the muffin mixture evenly between the 12 cups
   in the muffin pan or the paper cases (they should be
   about two-thirds full). Bake in a preheated oven,
   200°C/400°F/Gas Mark 6, for 25 minutes or until risen
   and golden. Remove the muffins from the oven and
   serve warm, or place them on a wire rack to cool.

dairy-free berry muffins

ingredients

makes 12

1 large baking apple, peeled,
    cored and thinly sliced
3 tbsp water
1 tsp allspice
2 tbsp sunflower or peanut oil,
    plus extra for oiling (if using)
225 g/8 oz plain white or
    wholewheat flour
1 tbsp baking powder
¼ tsp salt
40 g/1½ oz wheatgerm
25 g/1 oz fresh raspberries
25 g/1 oz fresh strawberries,
    hulled and chopped
6 tbsp maple syrup
175 ml/6 fl oz apple juice

method

1 Place the sliced apple and the water in a saucepan and bring to the boil. Reduce the heat and stir in half of the allspice, then cover the pan and simmer, stirring occasionally, for 15–20 minutes or until the water has been absorbed. Remove the pan from the heat and cool. Transfer the apple mixture to a food processor and blend until smooth.

2 Lightly oil a 12-cup muffin pan with a little sunflower oil, or line the pan with 12 muffin paper cases.

3 Sift the flour, baking powder, salt and the remaining allspice into a mixing bowl, then stir in the wheatgerm.

4 In a separate bowl, mix the raspberries, strawberries, maple syrup, remaining oil, puréed apple and apple juice together. Add the fruit mixture to the flour mixture and gently stir until just combined. Do not overstir the mixture – it is fine for it to be a little lumpy.

5 Divide the muffin mixture evenly between the 12 cups in the muffin pan or the paper cases (they should be about two-thirds full). Transfer to a preheated oven, 190°C/375°F/Gas Mark 5, and bake for 25 minutes or until risen and golden. Remove from the oven and serve warm, or place them on a wire rack to cool.

fruity muffins

ingredients

makes 10

275 g/10 oz self-raising
    wholewheat flour
2 tsp baking powder
2 tbsp brown sugar
85 g/3 oz no-soak dried apricots,
    finely chopped
1 banana, mashed with
    1 tbsp orange juice
1 tsp finely grated orange rind
300 ml/10 fl oz skimmed milk
1 large egg, beaten
3 tbsp sunflower or peanut oil
2 tbsp rolled oats
fruit spread, honey or maple
    syrup, to serve

method

1 Line 10 cups of a 12-cup muffin pan with muffin paper
   cases. Sift the flour and baking powder into a mixing
   bowl, adding any husks that remain in the sieve. Stir in
   the sugar and chopped apricots.

2 Make a well in the centre and add the mashed banana,
   orange rind, milk, beaten egg and oil. Mix together
   well to form a thick mixture and divide the mixture
   evenly between the muffin cases.

3 Sprinkle with a few rolled oats and bake in a preheated
   oven, 200°C/400°F/Gas Mark 6, for 25–30 minutes until
   well risen and firm to the touch or until a toothpick
   inserted into the centre comes out clean.

4 Remove the muffins from the oven and place them on
   a wire rack to cool slightly. Serve the muffins while still
   warm with a little fruit spread, honey or maple syrup.

cranberry muffins

ingredients

makes 10

175 g/6 oz self-raising
    white flour
55 g/2 oz self-raising
    wholewheat flour
1 tsp ground cinnamon
½ tsp bicarbonate of soda
1 egg, beaten
70 g/2½ oz thin-cut orange
    marmalade
150 ml/5 fl oz skimmed or
    semi-skimmed milk
5 tbsp corn oil
115 g/4 oz peeled, cored and
    finely diced eating apple
115 g/4 oz fresh or frozen
    cranberries, thawed if frozen
1 tbsp rolled oats
freshly squeezed orange juice,
    to serve

method

1 Line a muffin pan with 10 muffin paper cases.

2 Place the white and wholewheat flours, cinnamon and bicarbonate of soda in a mixing bowl and combine thoroughly.

3 Make a well in the centre of the flour mixture. In a separate bowl, blend the egg with the marmalade until well combined. Beat the milk and oil into the egg mixture, then pour into the dry ingredients, stirring lightly. Do not overmix – the mixture should be slightly lumpy. Quickly stir in the apple and cranberries.

4 Spoon the mixture evenly into the paper cases and sprinkle a little oats over each muffin. Bake in a preheated oven, 200°C/400°F/Gas Mark 6, for 20–25 minutes or until well risen and golden, and a skewer inserted into the centre of a muffin comes out clean.

5 Lift out the muffins and transfer onto a wire rack. Cool for 5–10 minutes, then peel off the paper cases and serve warm with glasses of freshly squeezed orange juice. These muffins are best eaten on the day they are made – any leftover muffins should be stored in an airtight container and consumed within 24 hours.

blueberry muffins

ingredients

makes 12

vegetable oil cooking spray,
    for oiling (if using)
225 g/8 oz plain flour
1 tsp bicarbonate of soda
¼ tsp salt
1 tsp allspice
115 g/4 oz caster sugar
3 large egg whites
3 tbsp low-fat margarine
150 ml/5 fl oz thick low-fat natural
    or blueberry-flavoured yogurt
1 tsp vanilla essence
85 g/3 oz fresh blueberries

method

1 Spray a 12-cup muffin pan with vegetable oil cooking
   spray, or line it with 12 muffin paper cases.

2 Sift the flour, bicarbonate of soda, salt and half of the
   allspice into a large mixing bowl. Add 6 tablespoons
   of the caster sugar and mix together.

3 In a separate bowl, whisk the egg whites together.
   Add the margarine, yogurt and vanilla essence and mix
   together well, then stir in the fresh blueberries until
   thoroughly mixed. Add the fruit mixture to the flour
   mixture, then gently stir until just combined. Do not
   overstir the mixture – it is fine for it to be a little lumpy.

4 Divide the muffin mixture evenly between the 12 cups
   in the muffin pan or the paper cases (they should be
   about two-thirds full). Mix the remaining sugar with
   the remaining allspice, then sprinkle the mixture over
   the muffins. Transfer to a preheated oven, 190°C/375°F/
   Gas Mark 5, and bake for 25 minutes or until risen and
   golden. Remove the muffins from the oven and serve
   warm, or place them on a wire rack to cool.

honey & lemon muffins

ingredients

makes 12

50 g/1¾ oz unrefined caster sugar
2 tbsp unsalted butter, melted
   and cooled slightly
150 ml/5 fl oz buttermilk
2 eggs, beaten
4 tbsp flower honey
finely grated rind of 1 lemon
   and juice of ½ lemon
225 g/8 oz plain flour
150 g/5½ oz oat bran
1½ tbsp baking powder

method

1 Line a 12-hole muffin pan with muffin paper cases.
   Put the sugar into a jug and add the butter, buttermilk,
   eggs, half the honey and lemon rind. Mix briefly
   to combine.

2 Sift the flour into a large mixing bowl, add the oat
   bran and baking powder, and stir to combine. Make
   a well in the centre of the flour mixture and add the
   buttermilk mixture. Quickly mix together – do not
   overmix; the mixture should be slightly lumpy.

3 Spoon the mixture into the paper cases and bake
   in a preheated oven, 180°C/350°F/Gas Mark 4, for
   25 minutes. Turn out onto a wire rack.

4 Mix the lemon juice with the remaining honey in a
   small bowl or jug and drizzle over the muffins while
   they are still hot. Let the muffins stand for 10 minutes
   before serving.

moist orange & almond muffins

ingredients

makes 12

2 oranges
about 100 ml/3½ fl oz milk
225 g/8 oz plain flour
1 tbsp baking powder
pinch of salt
115 g/4 oz caster sugar
55 g/2 oz ground almonds
2 eggs
6 tbsp sunflower oil or 85 g/3 oz
    butter, melted and cooled
½ tsp almond extract
40 g/1½ oz demerara sugar

method

1 Line a 12-hole muffin pan with 12 paper cases. Finely grate the rind from the oranges and squeeze the juice. Add enough milk to make the juice up to 250 g/9 fl oz, then stir in the orange rind. Sift together the flour, baking powder and salt into a large bowl. Stir in the caster sugar and ground almonds.

2 Place the eggs in a bowl and beat lightly, then beat in the orange mixture, oil and almond extract. Make a well in the centre of the dry ingredients, pour in the liquid ingredients and mix. Spoon the mixture into the paper cases. Sprinkle the demerara sugar over the tops.

3 Bake in a preheated oven, 200°C/400°F/Gas Mark 6, for 20 minutes, or until well risen, golden brown and firm to the touch. Leave to cool in the tin for 5 minutes, then serve warm or transfer to a wire rack to cool completely.

spiced carrot cake muffins

ingredients

makes 12

2 tbsp sunflower or peanut oil, plus extra for oiling (if using)

100 g/3½ oz plain white flour

100 g/3½ oz plain wholewheat flour

1 tsp bicarbonate of soda

¼ tsp salt

1 tsp ground cinnamon

½ tsp ground ginger

2 tbsp caster sugar

2 large egg whites

5 tbsp skimmed or semi-skimmed milk

225 g/8 oz canned pineapple chunks in juice, drained, chopped and mashed

250 g/9 oz carrots, grated

40 g/1½ oz sultanas

40 g/1½ oz shelled walnuts, chopped

topping

225 g/8 oz low-fat soft cheese

1½ tbsp caster sugar

1½ tsp vanilla essence

1½ tsp ground cinnamon

method

1 Oil a 12-cup muffin pan with sunflower oil, or line it with 12 muffin paper cases. Sift both flours, bicarbonate of soda, salt, cinnamon and ginger into a mixing bowl. Add the caster sugar and mix together.

2 In a separate bowl, whisk the egg whites together, then mix in the milk and remaining oil. Add the mashed pineapple, the carrots, sultanas and walnuts and stir together gently. Add the fruit mixture to the flour mixture and stir gently until just combined. Do not overstir the mixture – it is fine for it to be a little lumpy.

3 Divide the muffin mixture evenly between the 12 cups in the muffin pan or the paper cases (they should be about two-thirds full). Transfer to a preheated oven, 190°C/375°F/Gas Mark 5, and bake for 25 minutes or until risen and golden, then cool on a wire rack.

4 While the muffins are in the oven, make the topping. Place the soft cheese in a mixing bowl with the caster sugar, vanilla essence and 1 teaspoon of the cinnamon. Mix together well, then cover with clingfilm and transfer to the refrigerator until ready to use.

5 When the muffins have cooled to room temperature, remove the topping from the refrigerator and spread some evenly over the top of each muffin. Lightly sprinkle over the remaining cinnamon and serve.

spiced wholewheat muffins

ingredients

serves 6

1 tbsp vegetable oil, plus
extra for oiling
125 g/4½ oz plain flour
½ tsp baking powder
55 g/2 oz wholewheat flour
½ tsp ground allspice
1 egg, lightly beaten
150 ml/5 fl oz buttermilk
1 tsp grated orange zest
1 tbsp freshly squeezed
orange juice
1 tsp low-sugar marmalade,
for glazing

filling

100 g/3½ oz no-fat Greek yogurt
1 tsp low-sugar marmalade
½ tsp grated orange zest
100 g/3½ oz fresh raspberries

method

1 Oil a 6-hole muffin pan lightly with vegetable oil.

2 Sift the plain flour with the baking powder into a large mixing bowl. Using a fork, stir in the wholewheat flour and allspice until thoroughly mixed. Pour in the oil and rub into the flour mixture with your fingertips.

3 In a separate bowl, mix the egg, buttermilk and orange zest and juice together, then pour into the centre of the flour mixture and mix with a metal spoon, being careful not to overmix – the mixture should look a little uneven and lumpy.

4 Spoon the mixture into the prepared pan to come about three-quarters of the way up the sides of each hole. Bake in a preheated oven, 160°C/325°F/Gas Mark 3, for 30 minutes or until golden brown and a skewer inserted into the centre of a muffin comes out clean. Remove from the oven and transfer to a wire rack. Brush with the marmalade and cool.

5 For the filling, mix the yogurt with the marmalade and orange zest. Cut the warm muffins through the centre and fill with the yogurt mixture and raspberries.

high-energy muffins

ingredients

makes 12

5 tbsp sunflower or peanut oil,
    plus extra for oiling (if using)
85 g/3 oz wholewheat flour
50 g/1¾ oz quick-cooking oats
40 g/1½ oz wheatgerm
2 tsp baking powder
1 tsp ground cinnamon
¼ tsp salt
40 g/1½ oz no-soak dried dates,
    pitted and chopped
55 g/2 oz sultanas
115 g/4 oz bran flakes
200 ml/7 fl oz milk
2 large eggs, beaten
5 tbsp honey
4 tbsp golden syrup
4 tbsp molasses

method

1 Oil a 12-cup muffin pan with sunflower oil, or line it with 12 muffin paper cases. Place the flour, oats, wheatgerm, baking powder, cinnamon and salt in a mixing bowl and mix together.

2 In a separate bowl, mix the dates, sultanas and bran flakes together. Pour in the milk and stir together, then stir in the beaten eggs, honey, golden syrup, molasses and remaining oil. Add the fruit mixture to the flour mixture and then gently stir until just combined. Do not overstir the mixture – it is fine for it to be a little lumpy.

3 Divide the muffin mixture evenly between the 12 cups in the muffin pan or the paper cases (they should be about two-thirds full). Transfer to a preheated oven, 190°C/375°F/Gas Mark 5, and bake for 20–25 minutes or until risen and golden. Remove the muffins from the oven and serve warm, or place them on a wire rack to cool.

sugarless chocolate muffins

ingredients

makes 12

4 tbsp sunflower or peanut oil,
    plus extra for oiling (if using)
225 g/8 oz plain flour
1 tbsp baking powder
1 tbsp cocoa powder
½ tsp allspice
2 large eggs
175 ml/6 fl oz unsweetened
    orange juice
1 tsp grated orange rind
40 g/1½ oz fresh blueberries

method

1 Oil a 12-cup muffin pan with sunflower oil, or line it with 12 muffin paper cases. Sift the flour, baking powder, cocoa and allspice into a large mixing bowl.

2 In a separate bowl, whisk the eggs and the remaining sunflower oil together. Pour in the orange juice, add the grated orange rind and the blueberries, and stir together gently to mix. Add the egg and fruit mixture to the flour mixture and then gently stir together until just combined. Do not overstir the mixture – it is fine for it to be a little lumpy.

3 Divide the muffin mixture evenly between the 12 cups in the muffin pan or the paper cases (they should be about two-thirds full). Transfer to a preheated oven, 200°C/400°F/Gas Mark 6, and bake for 20 minutes or until risen and golden. Serve the muffins warm, or place them on a wire rack to cool.

index